ALEXANDER WILLIAM EMERSON

# SCHEMES

*The Greatest Operations of World War II*

*Copyright © 2023 by Alexander William Emerson*

*All rights reserved. No part of this publication may be reproduced, stored or transmitted in any form or by any means, electronic, mechanical, photocopying, recording, scanning, or otherwise without written permission from the publisher. It is illegal to copy this book, post it to a website, or distribute it by any other means without permission.*

*Alexander William Emerson has no responsibility for the persistence or accuracy of URLs for external or third-party Internet Websites referred to in this publication and does not guarantee that any content on such Websites is, or will remain, accurate or appropriate.*

*Although the publisher and the author have made every effort to ensure that the information in this book was correct at press time and while this publication is designed to provide accurate information in regard to the subject matter covered, the publisher and the author assume no responsibility for errors, inaccuracies, omissions, or any other inconsistencies herein and hereby disclaim any liability to any party for any loss, damage, or disruption caused by errors or omissions, whether such errors or omissions result from negligence, accident, or any other cause. Neither the author nor the publisher shall be liable for any damages arising therefrom.*

*First edition*

*This book was professionally typeset on Reedsy.
Find out more at reedsy.com*

*For Stella*

# Contents

| | |
|---|---|
| *Foreword* | iii |
| Introduction | 1 |
| Operation Fall Gelb (Case Yellow or the German Invasion of... | 3 |
| Operation Dynamo (Evacuation at Dunkirk) | 8 |
| Operation Catapult (Seizure of French Ships and the Attack... | 13 |
| Operation Sonnenblume (Germans Arrive in North Africa) | 19 |
| Operation 25 (Invasion of Yugoslavia) | 25 |
| Operation AI (The Japanese Sneak Attack on Pearl Harbor) | 29 |
| Operation Paukenschlag (German U-Boats' Second Happy Time) | 38 |
| Operation Barbarossa (Germany's Invasion of the Soviet... | 42 |
| Operation R (Battle of Rabaul) | 57 |
| Operation Chariot (St. Nazaire Raid) | 61 |
| Operation Anthropoid (Assassination of Reinhard Heydrich,... | 66 |
| Operation MI (Battle of Midway, 1942) | 69 |
| Operation Jubilee (Raid at Dieppe) | 83 |
| Operation Torch (Allied invasion of North Africa) | 90 |
| Operation Uranus (Soviet Counterattack in Stalingrad) | 97 |
| Operation I-Go (Japanese Counterattack in the Solomons and... | 102 |
| Operation Mincemeat (Deception Campaign for the Invasion of... | 107 |
| Operation Vengeance (The Plot to Kill Admiral Yamamoto) | 112 |
| Operation Chastise (The Dambusters Raid) | 119 |
| Operation Citadel (The Battle of Kursk) | 127 |
| Operation Husky (Allied invasion of Sicily) | 134 |
| Operation Eiche (The Gran Sasso Raid or the Rescue of Benito... | 142 |
| Operation Fortitude (Allied Deception Campaign for Normandy... | 149 |

| | |
|---|---|
| Operation Jericho (Amiens Prison Raid) | 157 |
| Operation Argument (Big Week or the Planned Destruction of... | 163 |
| Operation U-Go (Japan's India Campaign) | 168 |
| Operation Ichi-Go (Japanese offensive in China) | 174 |
| Operation Diadem (Battle of the Liri Valley or the Fourth... | 180 |
| Operation Overlord (D-Day or the Allied invasion of... | 184 |
| Operation Bagration (Soviet Offensive on the Eastern Front) | 203 |
| Operation Market Garden (Allied Airborne Operation in the... | 215 |
| Operation Bodenplatte (The Luftwaffe's Last Stand) | 223 |
| Operation Varsity (Allied Airborne Assault on Germany, Part... | 228 |
| Operation Amherst (Airdrop of Mainly French Commandos in the... | 235 |
| Operation Ten-Go (The Battleship Yamato's Last Stand) | 238 |
| Notable Canceled Operations | 244 |
| *Images* | 250 |
| *Also by Alexander William Emerson* | 262 |

# Foreword

Operations are the heartbeat of wars, shaping the destiny of nations and the course of history. In World War II, operations emerged as the fulcrum upon which victory pivoted. They weren't mere maneuvers; they were the catalysts that unleashed change, the strategies that rearranged borders, and the audacious plans that decided the fates of millions.

Within these pages, we'll delve into the operations that molded the conflict. Tales of ingenuity, heroism, and sacrifice will unfold, reflecting both humanity's darkness and the light of selfless acts for strangers' sake. Embark on this odyssey through World War II's defining operations.

# Introduction

The clock on the wall continued its relentless march, each tick resonating through the quiet study where General Dwight D. Eisenhower sat alone. Hours earlier, he had given the fateful signal to launch Operation Overlord, and now, in the depths of the night, he was left in agonizing suspense. Reports had yet to reach him, and the silence surrounding the fate of the mission was deafening.

An air of uncertainty hung heavy in the room, suffocating Eisenhower's thoughts. He looked around the maps and plans — reminders of the tremendous responsibility he bore. Will the invasion breach the mighty Atlantic Wall, or will the Germans push his forces back to the sea?

As the hours dragged on, Eisenhower's mind became a battlefield of doubts and fears. Had he done enough to ensure the safety and success of the brave soldiers under his command? Had he overlooked critical details in the meticulous planning? The burden of command weighed on him, the weight of thousands of lives resting on his shoulders, their fates entwined with his decisions.

Outside the confines of his study, the world was still and quiet, as if holding its breath in anticipation of the news. The distant sounds of sirens and explosions, muffled by the thick walls, were an ominous reminder of the chaos unfolding in some distant corner of the world. But here, in the solitude of his sanctuary, Eisenhower was left to grapple with the unknown, his mind racing with countless scenarios, each more haunting than the last.

He paced the room, seeking solace in motion, but finding none. The darkness outside matched the uncertainty within, and his heart pounded in his chest, a constant reminder of the gravity of the moment. With every passing minute, the lack of information gnawed at him, testing his resolve, his faith in the meticulous planning and preparation that had gone into the operation.

Alone with his thoughts, Eisenhower faced the prospect of not knowing. The phone remained ominously silent, leaving him to confront the void of information. In the silence, he questioned the very core of his being—a leader bound to his responsibilities, yet paralyzed by his lack of control over the unfolding events.

As the night wore on, a sense of helplessness settled upon him. He had steeled himself for the uncertainty of war, but the reality of it was crushing. The fate of the free world was being decided on distant shores, and he, the leader of the Allied forces, was left to grapple with his own vulnerability.

In the solitude of his study, surrounded by the tools of his trade, Eisenhower found himself stripped bare of rank and uniform. He was just a man, consumed by a sense of duty, haunted by the lives under his command. In the depths of that night, he understood the true weight of leadership, the cost of command.

As the first rays of dawn filtered through the curtains, Eisenhower's mind remained clouded by the unknown. He would face the coming day with the same unwavering resolve that had brought him to this moment, even without the answers he sought. The war would continue, and he would find strength hoping the courage and determination of his forces had prevailed. Alone, yet not alone, he would wait for news, prepared to face whatever outcome fate had in store.

# Operation Fall Gelb (Case Yellow or the German Invasion of France and the Low Countries)

*May 10 to June 20, 1940*

**Belligerents:** Germany vs. France, the United Kingdom, Belgium, and the Netherlands

**Objective:** Conquest of France, Belgium, Luxembourg, and the Netherlands

**Outcome:** Conquest of France, Belgium, Luxembourg, and the Netherlands

## Background

Fall Gelb, also known as Case Yellow or Operation Sichelschnitt, stands as a pivotal German military operation executed during World War II. Launched on May 10, 1940, it marked the invasion of France and the Low Countries by Nazi Germany, mainly orchestrated by General Erich von Manstein, earning it the moniker of the "Manstein plan."

In this strategic blueprint, the key thrust of the invasion aimed to pass through the seemingly impenetrable Ardennes in southern Belgium, and then proceed along the Somme valley. The conventional military mindset had dismissed the Ardennes Forest as too dense and impassable, leading French Army leaders, including Chief of Staff Maurice Gamelin, to believe that the static defense system of the Maginot Line along the Franco-German border would deter any German assault.

Tragically for the Allies, the Maginot Line did not extend to Belgium, where the German attack eventually originated. As a result, the defense against the invasion proved insufficient, with minimal fortifications and reserve divisions available to counter the swift German offensive. The successful execution of Fall Gelb highlighted the crucial importance of adaptability and the risks of underestimating enemy strategies in wartime.

During that period, the French possessed a larger and, on paper, a more formidable army compared to the Germans. Some German commanders, such as General Hasso von Manteuffel, even acknowledged that France had more and better tanks. However, unlike the Germans, the French tanks were dispersed rather than concentrated. The German forces strategically organized their armor as the spearhead, leading the rest of the army, employing the blitzkrieg strategy—a lightning-fast and potent approach of striking against the enemy. Leveraging innovative tactics and capitalizing on French over-confidence, the Germans successfully broke through the French and British lines.

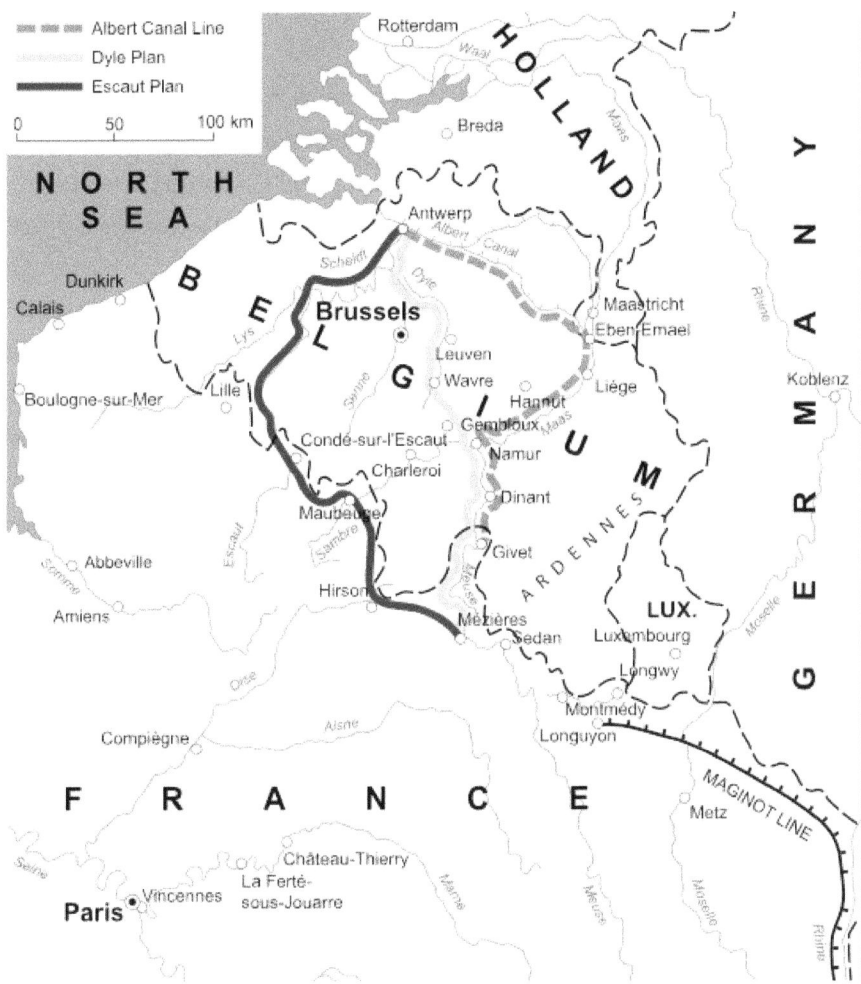

*Figure 1.* Planned Allied Defense of France. Note the mainly undefended area in the Ardennes.

## Operation

The invasion began with the German forces launching near-simultaneous and swift attacks on the Netherlands, France, Luxembourg, and Belgium. Using their superior armor, air power, and adept combined arms tactics, they stunned the defenses of these countries, aiming to execute a pincer movement to encircle and isolate the Allied forces.

As the German forces advanced on other fronts, they confronted the formidable and heavily fortified Maginot Line, constructed by the French along their border with Germany. Outflanking this defense system, the Germans relentlessly pushed back the Allied forces, causing them to retreat. Before long, the Germans encircled the rushing Allied forces, including France's best and most modern military units.

On May 19, the French Premier Paul Reynaud replaced Gamelin with Maxime Weygand as head of the French army. But the transition took time and then it was too late.

This operation is noteworthy for the insubordination of the German Panzer commanders including Hans Guderian. Instead of stopping and waiting for the rest of the army, they quickly advanced to the English Channel. This led to the capture of Boulogne and the sieges of Calais and later of Lille.

Manstein's plan had cut the Allied army into two and was in danger of complete annihilation. On June 22, 1940 just six weeks after the invasion, France surrendered.

*Figure 2.* German Panzers advancing through the forest

## Aftermath

Operation Fall Gelb culminated in the evacuation of the British Expeditionary Force from Dunkirk, as the German forces closed in on the French coast. The successful execution of the operation led to the fall of France, with the signing of an armistice on June 22, 1940.

This operation showed the effectiveness of the blitzkrieg strategy and the German military's ability to swiftly defeat well-fortified and numerically superior forces. It established German dominance in Western Europe and marked a significant turning point in the early stages of World War II.

# Operation Dynamo (Evacuation at Dunkirk)

*26 May to 04 June 1940*

**Belligerents:** England and France vs. Germany

**Objective:** Evacuate the British Expeditionary Force and their allies trapped at Dunkirk.

**Outcome**: Over 338,000 Allied soldiers evacuated, much more than the 30,000 that Prime Minister Winston Churchill expected. About a third of the evacuated soldiers were French, most of whom were returned to parts of then unoccupied France to continue the fight.

Operation Dynamo, also known as the Miracle of Dunkirk, was a military operation carried out during World War when the Allies evacuated over 338,000 Allied soldiers from the beaches and harbor of Dunkirk in Northern France.

## Background

Following the German invasion of France, the Allied forces from England, France, and Belgium found themselves surrounded and trapped by the advancing German army. The situation became increasingly dire, with the possibility of a total Allied defeat and the capture or annihilation of their troops.

Around May 21, BEF commander General Viscount Gort realized he had to evacuate his army across the channel. He chose Dunkirk, the closest viable port.

In response, Operation Dynamo was started to rescue the stranded soldiers. It involved a massive coordinated effort by the British Royal Navy, along with civilian vessels and boats, to evacuate the Allied troops from the beaches of Dunkirk. Time was not on their side and a determined push by the Germans could easily get past their defensive perimeter.

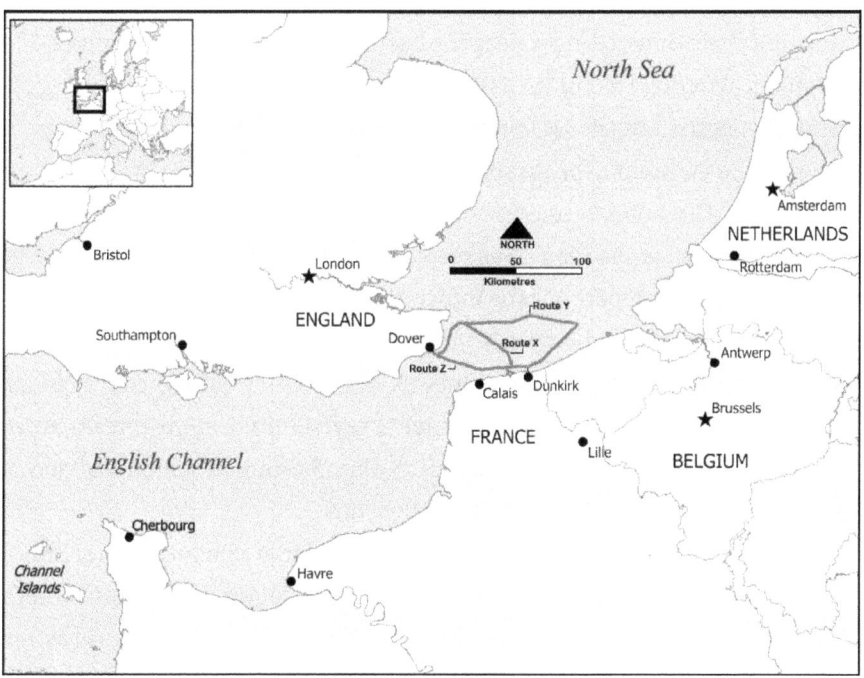

*Figure 3.* Shipping routes for Operation Dynamo.

## Operation

Remarkably, on May 23, Generaloberst Gerd von Rundstedt, commander of Army Group A, issued an astonishing order for the German Army to halt their advance. Fears arose that the German army's supplies had reached critical levels, prompting Hitler to assign destroying the Allied army to the Luftwaffe. Unfortunately, the Luftwaffe's infrastructure had not kept pace with the rapid German advance, causing logistical challenges, such as the JU-88s having to operate from airfields about 170 kilometers away, significantly reducing their time to linger near the beaches and the English Channel. The Germans also diverted units to Operation Paula, aimed at eliminating the remnants of the French Air Force.

While the German army grappled with logistics and remained in a state of idleness, the Allies seized the opportunity to construct defensive works, mainly for rearguard action. This respite also provided the Allied forces with precious time to prepare for the impending Battle of Dunkirk.

Between May 26 and June 4, 1940, an armada of over 800 naval vessels, comprising destroyers, minesweepers, and civilian ships, courageously traversed the perilous English Channel to reach Dunkirk. Despite enduring relentless German air attacks and artillery bombardment, their mission was to rescue the stranded soldiers on the beaches.

The evacuation encountered several formidable challenges, including shallow waters that hindered larger ships from reaching the shore directly. Smaller vessels had to shuttle soldiers from the beaches to the awaiting ships. While most soldiers adhered to discipline, some swam out of turn to reach the incoming vessels.

The evacuation prioritized the safety of the soldiers, resulting in them leaving behind a significant amount of equipment. Approximately five times the amount they had in England was abandoned, including nearly 900 field guns, 500 anti-aircraft guns, 700 tanks, and over 60,000 motor vehicles, apart from the massive ammunition cache.

### *French Rearguard Action*

An often overlooked part of the operation is the role of the French in making the evacuation a success.

From May 28 to 31, about 40,000 French soldiers fought a delaying action during the siege of Lille against a strong German army, which included 3 armored divisions. The French manned the defensive lines and held against superior numbers and armor.

As the British and their Allies evacuated, remnants of the French army kept the Germans at bay and bought them time. After their surrender, the Germans later sent most of these French soldiers to labor camps.

*Figure 4.* Steam Ferry SS Mona Queen sinks after hitting a mine.

## Aftermath

Despite these obstacles, the evacuation proved to be a remarkable success. Over the course of nine days, approximately 338,000 Allied soldiers, including British, French, and Belgian troops, were evacuated from Dunkirk. The operation surpassed all expectations and became a symbol of resilience and determination in the face of overwhelming odds.

As Dynamo went on, the Royal Air Force and the Luftwaffe waged an air war. The British lost 145 airplanes, including 42 Spitfires. By comparison, the Germans lost 156 planes.

After Operation Dynamo, they shipped most of the evacuated French troops back to France along with other British soldiers. The Allies wanted to continue the fight until France fell completely. But then Lieutenant-General (later Field Marshal) Alan Brooke convinced Churchill to evacuate all British forces, along with some Allied soldiers and civilians. This became Operation Aerial where many of the French soldiers evacuated formed Charles de Gaulle's Free French Army.

# Operation Catapult (Seizure of French Ships and the Attack on Mers-el-Kébir)

*July 3, 1940*

**Belligerents:** United Kingdom vs. France

**Objective:** After France surrendered to Germany, the British aimed to neutralize or destroy neutral French ships and prevent them from falling into German hands.

**Outcome:** Destruction of the French fleet in the Mediterranean port of Mers-el-Kébir on the coast of French Algeria. It also revived Anglophobia in France and strained the relationship between the two close allies.

## Background

Operation Catapult was a series of actions carried out by the British Royal Navy against the French Navy during World War II. It took place in July 1940, shortly after the fall of France to German forces and the establishment of the Vichy government in unoccupied France.

## SCHEMES

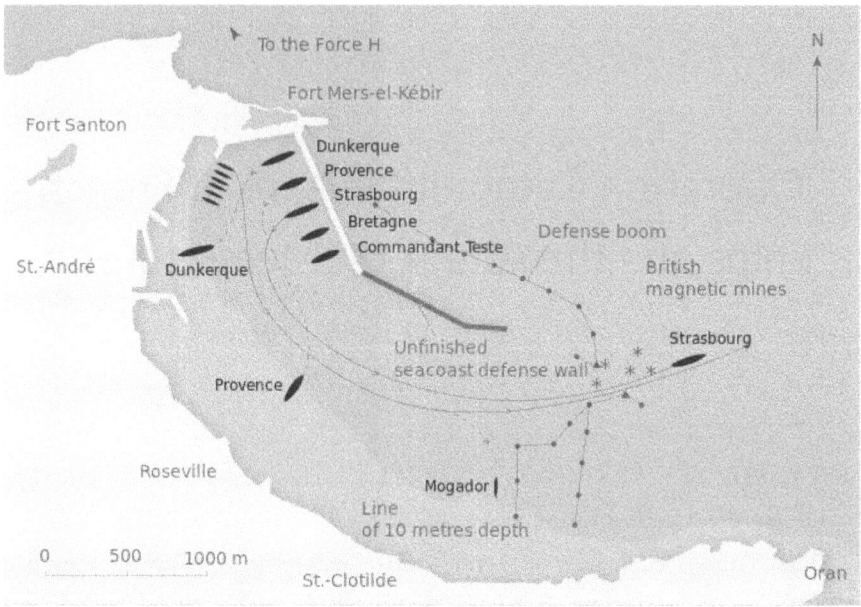

*Figure 5.* French fleet at Mers-el-Kébir.

Following the armistice between France and Germany, concerns arose regarding the fate of the French fleet. The British were apprehensive that the powerful French Navy, including capital ships and submarines, could fall into German hands or be used against the Allies. At this time, the Royal Navy still reigned supreme, but the combination of Germany's and France's Navy was an existential threat to the empire's survival.

In response to this perceived threat, the British initiated Operation Catapult. The operation included a series of diplomatic negotiations, seizures of French ships, and, sometimes, the use of force.

*Figure 6.* A French Battleship (either the Dunkerque or the Strasbourg) under fire during Operation Catapult.

## Operation

On July 3, the English captured French ships stationed in Plymouth and Portsmouth. Among the ships taken were the Surcouf, which was the biggest submarine in the world at the time, old battleships Paris and Courbet, 2 destroyers, four other submarines, eight torpedo boats, and other smaller ships.

Despite confusion and resentment by the French, the boarding of these ships was relatively peaceful. There were casualties, though, as three Royal Navy personnel and a French sailor died. Crew Members either joined the Free French forces or repatriated back to France.

At Alexandria and Mers-el-Kébir, the British planned to do the same and presented the major French squadrons four options:

1. Steam to British ports and join the fight on the British side
2. Bring the ships to a British port or the French Caribbean. Crews will be repatriated and ships will be returned at the end of the war.
3. Disarm the ships and remain in port.
4. Sink their own ships.

It was strongly implied that rejecting these options meant the British would attack.

At Alexandria, French Admiral René-Émile Godfroy complied with the British demands. He agreed to disarm his fleet and stay in port until the end of the war. Among the ships disarmed were the battleship Lorraine, the heavy cruiser Suffren and three modern light cruisers.

At Mers-el-Kébir French Admiral Marcel-Bruno Gensoul responded differently.

The negotiations began badly as the British sent Captain Cedric Holland to deliver the message to Admiral Gensoul. Holland is the captain of the aircraft carrier Ark Royal and the former liaison with the French admiralty. The British commander, Admiral James Somerville hoped that Holland's cordial and familiar relationship with the French would avoid bloodshed. Instead, Gensoul felt insulted that "only" a captain was sent to talk to him.

Gensoul later sent a telegram to his superiors at the new Vichy government telling them about the British presence and their ultimatum. Significantly, he mentioned that the only options were whether the French or the British would sink the ships. He didn't mention the option to sail and join the Allies.

The French rejected the British demands but maintained that they would never let the Axis use the ships against the Allies. However, reconnaissance showed that French ships at Algiers were on the move and probably sailing for Mers-el-Kébir. The British task force wasn't sure whether they would join the Allies or attack them.

Still, both Gensoul and Holland were desperate to avoid bloodshed. Gensoul told Holland that he had secret instructions from French Admiral Darlan to scuttle his ships or sail to North America if the Nazis tried to take them. However, this answer was not enough for the British. Britain was not taking any chances.

As the deadline arrived, Somerville ordered his ships to attack. The French ships, located in a narrow harbor were sitting ducks. One of the French battleships, the Bretagne was sunk with 1012 lives lost. The battleship Dunkerque was damaged while Strasbourg escaped. Both ships will eventually reach Toulon.

## Aftermath

Operation Catapult was a highly controversial and tragic event in Anglo-French relations. The attack stirred powerful emotions and caused significant resentment among the French population. Marshal Philippe Pétain, head of the new Vichy government cut off diplomatic ties with the British.

Two years later, when the Allies landed in Africa, Hitler attempted to seize the ships for use mainly at the Mediterranean theater. The French proved they were true to their word, that they would never let the Axis use their ships against the Allies. On November 27, 1942, they scuttled 77 ships including the two capital ships that survived the attack on Mers-el-Kébir, the battleships Dunkerque and Strasbourg.

Finally, the attack showed the ruthlessness of Britain in persecuting the war. It was a clear sign that they had no intention to surrender and would fight no matter the cost.

SCHEMES

***Figure 7.*** The French battleship Bretagne sinks.

# Operation Sonnenblume (Germans Arrive in North Africa)

***February 6 to May 25 1941***

*Belligerents:* Germans and Italians vs. the United Kingdom

*Objective:* Save Italy's North African Campaign

*Outcome:* The Afrika Korps' arrival improved the Axis' fortunes in North Africa. This would continue until the Second Battle of El Alamein.

Operation Sonnenblume also known as Operation Sunflower refers to the sending of German reinforcements to North Africa in 1941. Italy's North African campaign was a disaster: the Italian 10th Army had been destroyed and Italy was in danger of losing the war in the theater.

## Background

The quick success of Germany against France led Mussolini to fear that the war might be over before Italy joined the fight, thus depriving him of spoils. He believed that the British and French empires were on the verge of collapse and their colonies were ripe for the taking. He also believed that it was time for a revival of the great Roman Empire.

So against the advice of some of his generals, on June 10, 1940 he declared war on England and France. Many of his generals believed Italy was not ready for the industrial level of warfare that was unfolding. Still, he set his eyes on the colonies in Africa, the Mediterranean, and more importantly, the Suez Canal.

On September 13, 1940, the commander of the Italian Army in North Africa, Marshal Rodolfo Graziani advanced to Egypt. His forces of over 236,000 men outnumbered the British about 2:1.

However, his infantry lacked the modern equipment of the British. Their best tank, the M13 had a powerful 47 mm gun, but could only move at nine miles an hour, reducing it to a semi-mobile artillery piece. The rest of the Italian tanks were simply no match for the British Matilda.

The same was true in the air as while Italy had a sizable Air Force, they were again no match for the British Hawker Hurricane.

By February 1941, The British stopped the Italian offensive and over 100,000 Italians had surrendered. The Italian adventure had turned to disaster and Hitler had to save his ally. Later that month, the first units of the new Deutsches Afrika Korps arrived.

OPERATION SONNENBLUME (GERMANS ARRIVE IN NORTH AFRICA)

*Figure 8.* Propaganda photo of Erwin Rommel helping to move his Škoda Superb Kfz 21 car, which had gotten stuck in the desert sand.

## Operation

General Erwin Rommel commanded the German forces and since it was an Italian campaign, and for diplomatic reasons, he was directed to serve under Italian General Gariboldi, the new Italian commander.

But Rommel was a subordinate only in name. He immediately organized the defense of western Libya. His army was beefed up by some of the best units in the Italian army—the Ariete and Trento armored divisions. He also reorganized the artillery and tank units for a more cohesive punch.

Rommel was ordered to be on the defensive and simply hold the line. But Rommel was an aggressive commander and when he saw weak points in the British defense, he attacked. First, he defeated them at El Agheila and placed Tobruk under siege. When Gariboldi tried to censure Rommel for disobeying orders, the latter simply ignored him.

Rommel continued to rack up one victory after another until British General Claude Auchinleck launched a counter-attack and recovered most of the territory taken by Rommel. He also ended the Axis' siege of Tobruk.

But Rommel attacked again and in June 1942 won the Battle of Gazala, which included the capture of Tobruk, capturing its large supplies, and inflicting over 50,000 casualties on the British. There was a real danger that capturing Egypt and the Suez Canal was just a matter of time.

Rommel's string of victories only ended with a stalemate during the First Battle of El Alamein.

# OPERATION SONNENBLUME (GERMANS ARRIVE IN NORTH AFRICA)

*Figure 9.* Afrika Korps in 1941.

## Aftermath

The Afrika Korps saved the Italian army from total destruction and humiliation. Rommel's leadership also proved that the Italian Army was capable if deployed correctly. The Ariete Armored Division fought as a single entity for the first time and had impressive victories, including at Bir el Gubi. Some historians even say that the inspired Ariete performed better than many units of the Afrika Korps.

However, Rommel's difficult supply issues and growing Allied strength eventually led to his defeat. After the Second Battle of El Alamein, the Axis' campaign in North Africa was effectively over.

# Operation 25 (Invasion of Yugoslavia)

*April 6 to 18, 1941*

**Belligerents**: Germany, Italy, Bulgaria, and Hungary vs. Yugoslavia, supported by the British and Greeks

**Objective:** Conquest of Yugoslavia

**Outcome:** Occupation of Yugoslavia

## Background

In 1941, under pressure from Hitler, Yugoslavia's Regent, Prince Paul, reluctantly agreed to join the Tripartite Pact. However, this decision triggered discontent among the country's military ranks. In response, the military launched a coup d'état on March 27, compelling the Regent to step down from power. In his place, they proclaimed 17-year-old King Peter II as the new ruler.

Perceiving this act as a personal insult, Hitler resolved to take severe action against Yugoslavia. Consequently, he launched Operation 25, also known as Unternehmer 25, intending to bring swift and devastating destruction upon the nation.

## Operation

German attacks began with the Luftwaffe's assault on the airfields of the Royal Yugoslav Air Force. Various planes of the Luftwaffe flew from airfields in Austria and Romania with 150 bombers and dive-bombers with a heavy fighter escort. The first wave of attacks quickly wiped out the Yugoslav Air force and its inadequate anti-aircraft defenses. The Germans lost two fighters while destroying 20 planes in the air and another forty-four on the ground. More importantly, this air attack knocked out the Yugoslav communication center. This impeded coordination in the Yugoslav army.

*Figure 10.* A destroyed Yugoslavian Renault NC tank

This air assault was followed by a three-pronged German attack on Belgrade. Soon attacks from the Italians, Bulgarians, and Hungarians followed.

As a result, by April 17, 1941, German forces had occupied key Yugoslav cities and strategic points, leading to the surrender of the Yugoslav government. The invasion of Yugoslavia allowed Germany to gain control over the country and establish a puppet government.

## Aftermath

After the surrender, the country was subdivided among the tripartite members—Germany, Hungary, Italy, and Bulgaria. The puppet Croatian state fell under the control of Germany and Italy.

Among the major factors in the quick defeat is the Yugoslav's decision to defend everything instead on focusing on key points. Some also claim that members of the fifth column—a group of sympathizers of the Axis, sabotaged the military.

While the country fell quickly, the Yugoslavs continued to fight the Axis occupation. The resistance, led by Josip Tito, was the most effective anti-Axis partisan group in World War 2.

## SCHEMES

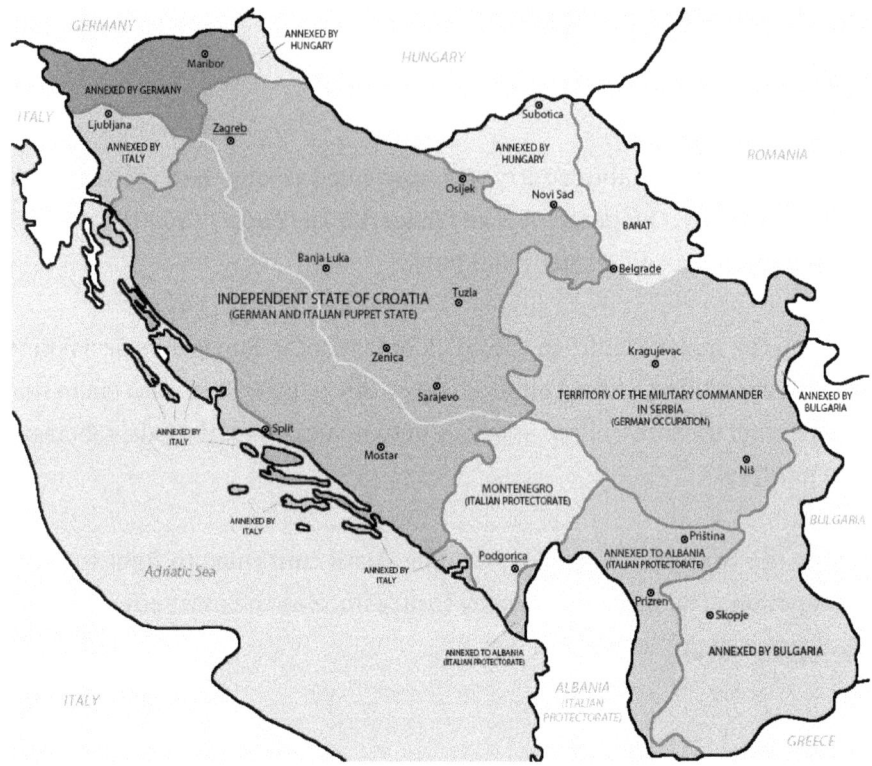

*Figure 11.* Occupation and partition of Yugoslavia, 1941.

# Operation AI (The Japanese Sneak Attack on Pearl Harbor)

***December 7, 1941***

**Belligerents:** Japan vs. the United States

**Objectives:** Disable the US Pacific Fleet and force the US to negotiate.

**Outcome:** All eight battleships were sank, but the aircraft carriers survived. The US declares war.

## Background

Operation AI, famously known as the Attack on Pearl Harbor, struck the United States Naval Base at Pearl Harbor, Hawaii, as a surprise military assault by the Imperial Japanese Navy on December 7, 1941.

The attack came after months of tense negotiations between the United States and Japan. With Japan's expanding empire in Asia raising concerns among the Allies, the US demanded Japan's withdrawal from China and French-Indochina. In return, they offered to unfreeze assets and lift embargos on essential raw materials like scrap metal and oil. The latter restriction was grave, as approximately 80% of Japan's oil supplies relied on imports from the US. With the embargo in place, the impending shortage of oil threatened to cripple the country's resources, amplifying the urgency and complexity of the situation.

For the Japanese government which was now controlled by extremist hawks, this was unacceptable. Japan felt that the United States' actions seriously threatened their strategic initiatives and are threats to the country's survival. If the US wouldn't give them oil, they'd get it elsewhere. They planned for the seizure of oil-rich resources in the Dutch East Indies, even though that would likely provoke the United States to join the war.

But America was not ready for war. At that time most Americans were averse to joining any war whether in Asia or Europe. Despite Britain's pleas, the US hadn't joined the fight against Nazi Germany. US President Franklin Roosevelt had to perform astute political maneuvers to provide the British aid.

Japan believed that their only chance for success lay in disabling the US Pacific fleet and simultaneously attacking multiple territories in Asia. Only then could they launch a successful invasion of the Dutch East Indies and get the resources they needed. A disabled US Navy in the Pacific meant that the Japanese Navy could conquer much of Southeast Asia without US interference.

They also believed that the US Navy would be paralyzed for at least half a year, giving them time to consolidate their gains and form a strong defensive perimeter for their new empire. They also expected the attacks to crush the morale of the US public and force the government to drop their demands and sue for peace.

To achieve all these, they set their sights on Pearl Harbor, primarily the battleships and aircraft carriers.

*Figure 12.* Photograph taken from a Japanese plane during the torpedo attack on ships moored on both sides of Ford Island shortly after the beginning of the Pearl Harbor attack.

## Operation

Japan was planning an earlier operation against the Soviet Union, Operation Kantokuen where they planned to seize territories in the Russian Far East. But this changed when the US enacted the total oil embargo. Suddenly, it was possible for the Japanese military to simply run out of fuel and their military would ground to a halt.

Admiral Isoroku Yamamoto, commander of the Japanese combined fleet, assumed responsibility for planning the operation. He began with intensified training and extensive intelligence gathering. Japan also learned valuable lessons from the British air attack on the Italian fleet at Taranto and trained their pilots accordingly.

To tailor the hardware for Pearl Harbor conditions, the Japanese made crucial modifications, notably enhancing the Type 91 aerial torpedo. With an anti-roll mechanism and a rudder extension, the torpedoes could operate in shallow waters, preventing them from sinking to the harbor bottom.

With the emperor's approval of the attack plan on November 5 and the final authorization on December 1, the Japanese armada, including six aircraft carriers—Akagi, Kaga, Sōryū, Hiryū, Shōkaku, and Zuikaku—departed Hittokapu Bay by November 26, carrying a formidable fleet of 408 aircraft.

The operation unfolded in two waves, with fighters supporting bombers and strategically targeting ground installations. The Japanese equipped bombers with torpedoes and bombs, specifically designed to devastate capital ships. Regrettably for Japan, they underestimated the duration of the war and consequently did not prioritize the shore repair facilities and oil depots.

*Figure 13.* USS Arizona under attack and about to sink.

## *Declaration of War*

Admiral Yamamoto wanted the attack to proceed thirty minutes after the declaration of war. But the official notice was only received an hour after the attacks began. This was similar to how the Russo-Japanese War began, when the Imperial Japanese Navy had already attacked the Imperial Russian Navy in the Battle of Port Arthur before Japan formally declared war.

## *American Response*

Ironically, the previous commander of Pearl Harbor, James Richardson was relieved of his post because he protested concentrating the naval assets on Pearl Harbor. He argued it would be Japan's first target in the event of war.

And in the early morning of December 7, the Japanese proved him right.

The radar station at Opana Point detected the initial wave of incoming aircraft, near Oahu's northern tip. However, the officer on duty mistakenly assumed it was just the scheduled arrival of B-17s, failing to recognize the impending danger.

Before the attack, there were also reports sent to high command about the presence of midget submarines and encounters with Japanese fighters. Unfortunately, these crucial reports were either ignored or arrived too late to be acted upon effectively.

Admiral Husband Kimmel, Commander-in-Chief of the US Pacific fleet, received the warning about the attack only after it had already concluded.

As the Japanese planes appeared in the sky, the staff at Pearl Harbor still believed they were friendlies. It wasn't until the bombs rained down on the ships that they realized the United States was under attack. The forces at Pearl Harbor began fighting back.

**Figure 14.** The destroyer USS Shaw exploding after raging fire detonated her forward magazine. The stern of the USS Nevada can be seen in the foreground.

### *Third Wave*

The captains of all the aircraft carriers were willing to launch their forces for a third wave, but Admiral Chuichi Nagumo decided against it. He felt that the third wave would face a much stronger defense and would not be as effective. He was also worried about his fuel condition.

This meant that shore facilities, a potential target in a third strike, were hardly damaged.

## Aftermath

There was euphoria in Japanese streets when news of the success at Pearl Harbor reached the public. But deep down, the Japanese leaders knew time was not on their side. They had to consolidate their gains, as it was a matter of time before America's industrial might would crush them.

The attack on Pearl Harbor resulted in the loss of 2,403 American lives and caused extensive destruction to the naval facilities and infrastructure. It shocked the American public and provoked a strong response from the United States, leading to a declaration of war against Japan the following day.

On December 11, 1941, Germany declared war on the US. Suddenly the United Kingdom was no longer alone.

The Japanese expected American morale to drop and the government to sue for peace. Instead, they got the reverse. After the attack, there was overwhelming public approval to go to war, and the US shifted to a war economy. More importantly, the shallow waters of Pearl Harbor allowed the salvaging and repair of four battleships. Japan's dreams of a quick war and negotiated peace were over.

**Figure 15.** A small boat rescues a seaman from the burning battleship USS West Virginia which is burning in the background.

# Operation Paukenschlag (German U-Boats' Second Happy Time)

**January to August 1942**

**Belligerents:** Germany vs. the United States

**Objective:** Attack US shipping in US waters

**Outcome:** German success. This operation accounted for about over one-fifth of all ships sunk by U-boats in World War 2

## Background

Operation Paukenschlag, also known as Operation Drumbeat, was a German submarine campaign carried out shortly after the US joined World War II. It took place in early 1942 and targeted shipping along the eastern coast of the United States.

During the early stages of the war, US convoys were vulnerable and lacked proper organization. The US Navy faced a shortage of suitable escort vessels, exacerbating the challenges of safeguarding the shipping lanes. Additionally, Admiral Ernest King, the US Navy Commander-in-Chief, ignored early British recommendations for assistance in protecting the ships, further adding to the difficulties in securing the convoys from German submarine attacks.

## Operation

In January 1942, Operation Paukenschlag commenced, with German U-boats assigned to patrol the waters off the eastern seaboard, specifically targeting the Gulf Stream, a vital route for shipping traffic. The primary aim was to disrupt the transportation of essential supplies supporting the Allied war effort, leading the U-boats to focus on merchant vessels, tankers, and other ships.

When the operation started, the Kriegsmarine faced a shortage of submarines with the required range to strike the US East Coast. Initially relying on the larger but fewer Type IX submarines, they later transitioned to the more common Type VII, equipped with enough range through refueling and resupply. But this initially small squad inflicted considerable damage.

**Figure 16.** The Allied tanker Dixie Arrow sinks after being torpedoes by the U-boat U-71.

The Allied ships' silhouettes against sky glow and coastal lights, made them vulnerable and easy targets for the U-boats. The abundance of such targets led to Kriegsmarine Commander Donitz criticizing one U-Boat commander for having sunk only one ship during his patrol.

However, the situation changed on May 14, 1942, when convoy escorts arrived, and by August, the second "happy time" for the U-boats had ended, as their effectiveness in attacking Allied ships decreased significantly.

## Aftermath

Aside from the tragic loss of lives, the Allies lost 609 ships totaling 3.1 million tons. The Germans only lost 22 U-boats.

Operation Paukenschlag highlighted the effectiveness of German submarine warfare and its ability to strike deep into enemy territory. It also showed the challenges faced by the United States early in the war in protecting its coastal waters.

*Figure 17.* The tanker Pennsylvania Sun burns after being torpedoed by U-571. The Pennsylvania Sun was saved and returned to service in 1943.

# Operation Barbarossa (Germany's Invasion of the Soviet Union)

**June 22, 1941 to January 7, 1942**

**Belligerents:** Germany, Romania, Finland, Italy, Hungary, and Slovakia vs. the Soviet Union

**Objectives:** Conquer the Soviet Union and repopulate it with Germans. Capture Russia's resources and its citizens for the war effort and slave labor, respectively.

**Outcome:** Despite initial rapid success, the operation floundered as winter came and the Russians regrouped.

Operation Barbarossa was the codename for the German invasion of the Soviet Union during World War II. It was launched on June 22, 1941, and marked the largest military offensive in history at that time. It was originally called Operation Fritz, but Hitler changed it to Barbarossa in honor of Frederick Barbarossa, the Holy Roman Emperor in the twelfth century.

Under the leadership of Adolf Hitler, Germany aimed to eliminate the Soviet Union as a political and military power, acquire its resources, and establish German dominance in Eastern Europe. The operation involved three German army groups, totaling over three million troops, along with their Axis allies, advancing along a vast front stretching from the Baltic Sea to the Black Sea.

*Figure 18. A German column led by a Panzer during the advance on Murmansk, July 1941.*

Operation Barbarossa was supposed to start five weeks earlier. However, the unforeseen necessity of invading Yugoslavia and the need to help their Italian Allies delayed the German offensive.

Despite this delay however, the Germans were confident they could conquer Ukraine and the European part of Russia, and reach the A-A Line before winter set in. This hypothetical line stretched from Arkhangelsk on the White Sea to the port city of Astrakhan. The Germans believed that majority of the Russian people and resources were within that territory.

Initially, the German advance met considerable success, as they caught the Soviet Union off guard. The Soviet forces suffered significant losses in men and equipment, and the German forces rapidly advanced, encircling and capturing vast numbers of Soviet troops. The cities of Minsk, Smolensk, and Kiev fell under German control.

However, as the German advance pushed deeper into the Soviet Union, the vastness of the territory, harsh weather, and fierce Soviet resistance slowed their progress. The Soviet Union mobilized its resources and launched a massive counteroffensive, particularly during the Battle of Moscow in the winter of 1941-1942.

## Background

In Mein Kampf, Hitler's autobiography and political manifesto, the German leader declared he would invade the Soviet Union. He believed that its vast land area was perfect for Lebensraum, a German concept of expansionism and Völkisch nationalism. Capturing this territory would ensure that future generations of Germans would have enough land and resources.

But in between the two wars, Germany and the Soviet Union had a strong and symbiotic relationship.

### *Treaty of Rapallo*

The 1922 Treaty of Rapallo between Weimar Germany and Soviet Russia annulled all mutual claims between the two nations, restored full diplomatic relations, and enhanced their trade relationship. This happened when both nations remained relative pariahs in the international community—Germany because of the First World War and Russia because of communism. This resulted in Germany being the main trading and diplomatic partner of Russia.

The crippling sanctions from the Treaty of Versailles also meant the Germans couldn't rebuild their military. To solve this, Russia offered facilities deep inside their territories and away from discovery by Treaty inspectors. In return, they got access to Germany's technical developments and assistance in building Russia's General Staff, which later suffered from Stalin's purges.

In April 1922, Junkers began building aircraft just outside Moscow. Krupp, the famous artillery manufacturer soon followed. In 1925, the Germans built a flying school where they trained the first pilots of the future Luftwaffe. Next the Germans built a tank school at Kazan and a chemical weapons facility at Saratov Oblast. This cooperation reached a peak in the early 1930s. In 1933 the Soviet Union abruptly terminated access to training sites at Lipetsk, Kama, and Tomka. This coincided with Hitler's rise to power and his heavy-handed measures against Soviet interests and citizens in Germany. After the Germans turned over factories to the Soviets, the latter began making variations of German weapons such as the Junkers bombers.

On the diplomatic front, the Soviet Union expanded its relationships with other nations. For the first time the country was diplomatically recognized by countries such as Spain, the United States, Hungary, Romania, Bulgaria, and Czechoslovakia. To top it all, they were admitted to the League of Nations in 1934.

Hitler also found new friends. In November 1936, Germany and Japan signed the Anti-Comintern Pact, a partnership against Communism.

This was a major reason the world was shocked in August 1939 when Germany and Russia signed the Molotov-Ribbentrop Pact—a non-aggression pact between the two countries. For Hitler, it meant that he could attack Poland without fearing a Russian attack. For Stalin, it temporarily gave him protection from German expansionism that England and France seemed helpless to stop. It also gave him time to strengthen his military.

After the Molotov-Ribbentrop pact, Japan distanced itself from Germany until September 1940 when they signed the Tripartite Pact with Italy, a defensive alliance.

Amidst all these, the Soviet Union continued to have trade relations with Germany. In 1940, the Soviets agreed to send 650 million Reichsmarks in raw materials (grain, oil, metal ores) in exchange for an equal amount of machinery, manufactured goods (synthetic material plants, ships, turrets, machine tools, and technology). This trade agreement helped Germany minimize the results of the British blockade in the early days of World War 2.

But similar to what the Germans did in 1939 with the Molotov-Ribbentrop pact; on April 13, 1941 Japan and the Soviet Union signed the Japanese-Soviet Non-aggression pact. This infuriated Hitler who was on the verge of launching Operation Barbarossa.

## Operation

Operation Barbarossa began with the bombing of Soviet-occupied Poland and an artillery barrage across the Russian front. Over three million men soon rolled into Soviet territory, at that time the largest invasion in human history. Air raids accompanied this, going as far as Kronstadt and Sevastopol.

*Figure 19.* German tanks advance during the Kesselschlacht near Wjasma. A Kesselschlacht is a blitzkrieg tactic where a strong force makes a frontal attack while forces on the flank execute a double envelopment. This forms a kessel or cauldron around the enemy.

Figures vary depending on the source, but historians agree that over 3.5 million troops from Germany and her allies attacked a 1,800-mile (2,896 km)-front. 148 divisions about 80% of the entire German army joined the attack. At the vanguard was the Panzer Corps with 3,400 tanks, supported by over 2,700 aircraft, over 7,000 artillery pieces, over 600,000 vehicles, and 600,000 horses. Hitler knew he had to apply overwhelming force if he hoped to win the battle quickly.

There were three army groups, each with a specific target:

1. Army Group North advanced from East Prussia and headed through

the Baltic states of Latvia, Lithuania, and Estonia and then capture Leningrad (now St. Petersburg). General Wilhelm Ritter von Leeb commanded this group.

2. Army Center advanced from north of the Pripet Marshes. Its primary objectives were Mińsk, Smolensk, and then Moscow. This was under General Fedor von Bock, supported by armored groups under General Heinz Guderian and General Hermann Hoth heading towards Moscow and Smolensk, respectively. Guderian and Hoth were two of Germany's most capable Panzer commanders.
3. Army Group South advanced from Southern Poland and would attack Ukraine towards Kiev and the Donbas industrial region. This was commanded by General Gerd von Rundstedt supported by an armored group under General Paul Ludwig Von Kleist heading towards Kiev.

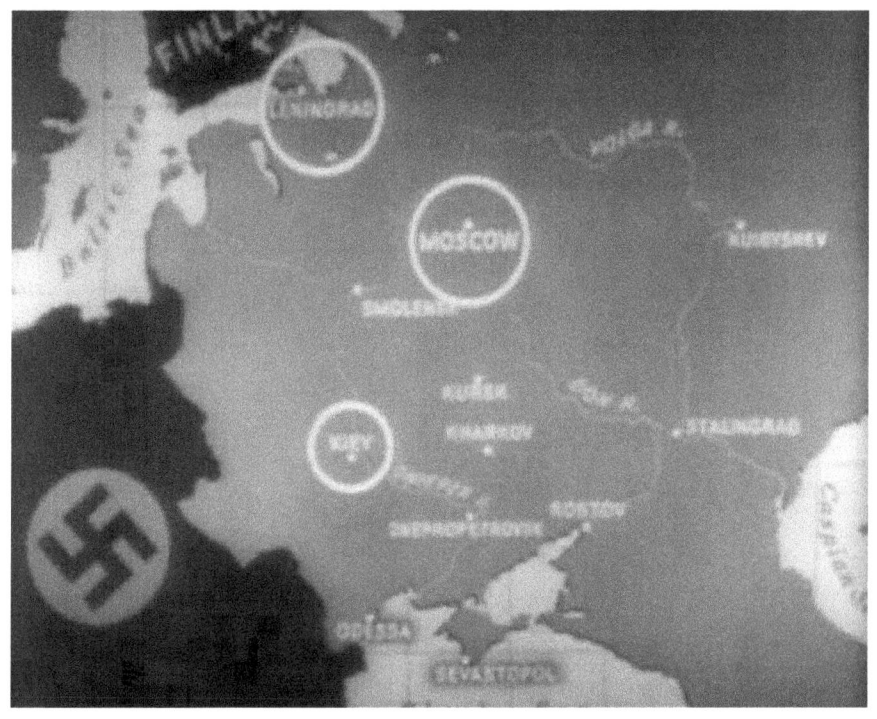

**Figure 20.** A still from the Why we Fight film series. It shows the three objectives of Operation Barbarossa.

Hitler expected to meet all these objectives in ten weeks. And in the early days of Barbarossa, he had to be confident about quickly knocking the Soviets out. Despite having about five million men and 23,000 (mostly obsolete and inoperable) tanks, Stalin was unprepared. His armies were dispersed, surprised, and soon routed.

As Hitler expected, all three Army groups made rapid progress, especially in the next three weeks.

During this period, Army Group North had advanced hundreds of miles. The Panzer groups of Guderian and Hoth encircled and captured over 600,000 soldiers and by July 27 had linked up at Smolensk. Among the three, Von Rundstedt faced the greatest resistance, but he pushed beyond Poland's original 1939 borders. On August 8, Army Group South reached the Dnieper River and placed the city under siege. Odessa surrendered on October 16, while Kiev fell on September 16.

**Figure 21.** Tanks from the 11th Panzer Division crossing the Dnieper River.

About ten weeks after the operations, wherein Hitler originally expected his army to rout the Russians, the German onslaught continued but began slowing down. They faced several problems.

1. First was logistics. They had exhausted their original supplies. Replenishment had to cover a longer distance before reaching the troops. Much of the army was expected to complement their food supply by living off the land, but the Soviets had adopted a scorched earth approach.

2. Second, the Soviets had began offering more organized and stubborn resistance. The Germans had also underestimated the size and resilience of the Red Army. Hitler didn't realize it at that time, but Stalin was sacrificing men and obsolete armor to buy him time.
3. Third, Hitler changed the strategic objectives of the war. Instead of an all-out drive towards Moscow, he wanted much of his army to focus on economic targets such as the industrial center of Kharkov, the Donbas, and later the oil fields of the Caucasus. He also directed some of his armies to pause their attack and redeploy some forces to the rear. These forces were to destroy pockets of resistance or encircled troops. These changes exasperated his generals.

Precious Russian lives were sacrificed, but these and Hitler's changing stances gave the Red Army time to strengthen their defenses. When Hitler ordered the attack on Moscow to resume, there were several new lines of defense and about an additional million defenders. This powerful defense, the Russian winter, and finally the counterattack on December 6 ended German hopes of threatening and capturing Moscow.

But the toll on lives was severe for the Russians. By December 1941, the Soviet Union had four million casualties, including about three million captured as POWs who were starving to death.

And on December 19, Hitler made probably the most consequential decision of the war in the East. He assumed personal control of the German Army, overruling his more experienced generals and ultimately leading Germany to defeat.

SCHEMES

*Figure 22.* German infantry in a burning village on the Eastern Front.

### *Air Battle*

The Germans destroyed over 2,000 Soviet planes on the first day of the invasion. By the third day, this figure had risen to over 3,900 against a German loss of only 78 aircraft. The Germans also attacked supply dumps, airfields, and command-and-control centers. This seriously disrupted the Soviet Union's ability to organize and mobilize.

### *Murder of Jews*

In the first weeks of the invasion, the Nazis killed Jewish women and children at random, but by the middle of August, they expanded this to all Jews.

As the Wehrmacht and its Allies advanced, four special operations divisions of the Einsatzgruppen scoured the country for Jews. The Einsatzgruppen comprised SS, police and auxiliaries mobilized from the local population. This group hunted the Jews and by the end of 1941, they had killed over half a million within the German-occupied territories.

**Figure 23.** Executions of Jews by German army mobile killing units (Einsatzgruppen) near Ivangorod Ukraine. The photo was mailed from the Eastern Front to Germany and intercepted at a Warsaw post office by a member of the Polish resistance collecting documentation on Nazi war crimes.

Among the most notorious of these murders happened in Babi Yar in Kiev. In September 1941, The Einsatzgruppen murdered 33, 771 Jews over two days. The site also witnessed the murder of gypsies and Soviet prisoners of war. They were taken in groups to massive pits and shot, with many were buried alive.

Dina Pronicheva was a survivor of the massacre. She would later testify about her ordeal during the Kiev war crimes trial.

By the winter of 1943 most of the Jews of Belorussia and almost half of the 2.5 million Jews of Ukraine had already been murdered.

### *Hitler Pauses the Advance to Moscow*

Army Group Center stopped its advance on Moscow partly to fix logistics, and to eliminate pockets of resistance at the Germans' rear.

The delay came with four complications for the Germans.

1. This delay enabled Russia to build new lines of defense around Moscow.
2. Late autumn and the Russian winter had also arrived, turning the roads into a muddy mess. The German army hospitals had more soldiers with frostbite than gunshot wounds.
3. Limited supplies from Britain had also begun to arrive giving the Russians just enough to stay in the fight.
4. In a strategic move, the field armies stationed along the eastern side of the Soviet Union were redeployed to Moscow. Although a non-aggression pact had been signed earlier between Japan and the Soviet Union, both sides harbored doubts about the other's commitment to the agreement. When Soviet intelligence agents finally verified that Japan had no intentions of launching an attack, Stalin made his move. The transferred troops were well trained, standing in stark contrast to the fresh recruits often sent to the Germans as cannon fodder.

On December 5, the Russians counter-attacked. One month later, they had pushed back the Germans over 100 kilometers (62 miles) from Moscow. This marked the end of Operation Barbarossa.

The following year, operations would resume but despite his generals' protests, Hitler insisted they change objectives. He wanted to attack the oil fields in the Caucasus and assault a city by the Volga named Stalingrad.

## Aftermath

Operation Barbarossa failed to capture many of its objectives, notably Moscow and Leningrad. This failure led Hitler to make one of the most consequential decisions of the war—taking personal command of the German Army and overruling his experienced generals. He continued to believe he was a great commander similar to the likes of Napoleon and especially Frederick the Great. This would have far-reaching consequences as his battlefield decisions and constantly shifting objectives would ultimately lead to disaster in the East. He was now fighting a war of attrition, something he didn't want and couldn't afford. As his armies grew weaker, the Soviets only became stronger.

Barbarossa and subsequent fighting in the Eastern Theater later proved to be a disaster for the Nazis. By the end of the war, Germany had lost about 4.5 million killed in battle and another 600,000 died in captivity. Russia suffered too and lost about 6.5 million men killed and another 3 million died while in captivity.

The Allies persisted in providing crucial supplies through initiatives like Lend-Lease, not only to support the Russian war effort but also to deter them from seeking a separate peace. Nevertheless, it was the Russians who bore the brunt of the casualties on the Eastern front. Had Stalin chosen to withdraw from the war, it would have significantly altered the dynamics of the Western front. Just as in World War 1, when peace with the Russians meant more enemy troops facing the British and French, a similar scenario in World War II would have resulted in a more formidable German Army in the West. This, in turn, could have made the landings at Normandy and other locations far more perilous and potentially doomed them to failure.

A successful Barbarossa could've delayed the liberation of Europe indefinitely.

# Operation R (Battle of Rabaul)

**January 23 to February 1942**
   ***Belligerents:*** Japan vs. Australia
   ***Objective:*** Invade Rabaul and transform it into a major Japanese base
   ***Outcome:*** Japanese successfully capture and fortify the Island.

Operation R, also known as the Rabaul Operation, was a Japanese military plan for the invasion of Rabaul in 1942. The battle was a strategic defeat for the Allies as the Japanese transformed Rabaul into a major base. Along with Truk, it became the linchpin of the Japanese presence in the Southern Pacific.

## Background

Rabaul, located on the eastern coast of New Britain Island in present-day Papua New Guinea, was a strategic stronghold for the Japanese in the Pacific theater during World War II. It served as a major base for their operations in the region and was heavily fortified.

   Under Operation R, the Japanese aimed to seize control of Rabaul and establish it as a key base to support their expansion in the South Pacific. The operation involved a combined force of Japanese navy, army, and air units.

## Operation

On January 23, 1942, the Japanese launched their invasion of Rabaul.

15,000 Japanese soldiers took on about 1,500 Australian defenders. A huge naval task force that included four fleet carriers also supported the Japanese.

The Japanese quickly overwhelmed the outnumbered and ill-prepared defenders. The Australians were forced to withdraw, and the Japanese gained control of Rabaul and its surrounding airfields.

The Japanese also executed about 160 prisoners, either with bayonets or guns. Many of the POWs would also die as they were being shipped to Japan when a US submarine sank the transport.

*Figure 24.* Reconnaisance photo of the Japanese naval base at Truk as ships and aircraft prepare for an assault on Rabaul in New Britain.

## Aftermath

The capture of Rabaul allowed the Japanese to establish a stronghold from which they could project their power in the Pacific. It served as a base for air operations and naval activities, and as a supply hub for their forces.

The airbase at Rabaul provided much of the air power and support in the region, including in the Guadalcanal and Bougainville campaigns. It is also noteworthy that Admiral Isoroku Yamamoto flew from Rabaul when P-38 lightnings intercepted his air convoy.

Since Rabaul was the biggest and most powerful Japanese base in the area, Allied planners bombed it continuously. But they did not launch an amphibious assault. Eventually, the Allies decided to isolate and bypass it during Operation Cartwheel, letting it in Douglas MacArthur's words, "wither in the vine."

When Japan surrendered in August 1945, there were still around 69,000 Japanese troops in Rabaul.

# Operation Chariot (St. Nazaire Raid)

*March 28, 1942*

**Belligerents:** United Kingdom vs. Germany

**Objective:** Destroy the St. Nazaire docks and deny its use to the Kriegsmarine.

**Outcome:** The raid rendered the dock unusable until the end of the war.

Operation Chariot, also known as the St. Nazaire Raid, was a British military operation during World War II. It took place on March 28, 1942, and aimed to disable the heavily fortified dry dock at St. Nazaire, France, which was used by the German Navy as a base for their largest battleships and U-boats. Destroying the dock also made the return of capital ships attacking Atlantic convoys too risky as they were in danger of meeting the Royal Navy's Home Fleet.

The operation is sometimes referred to as "The Greatest Raid."

SCHEMES

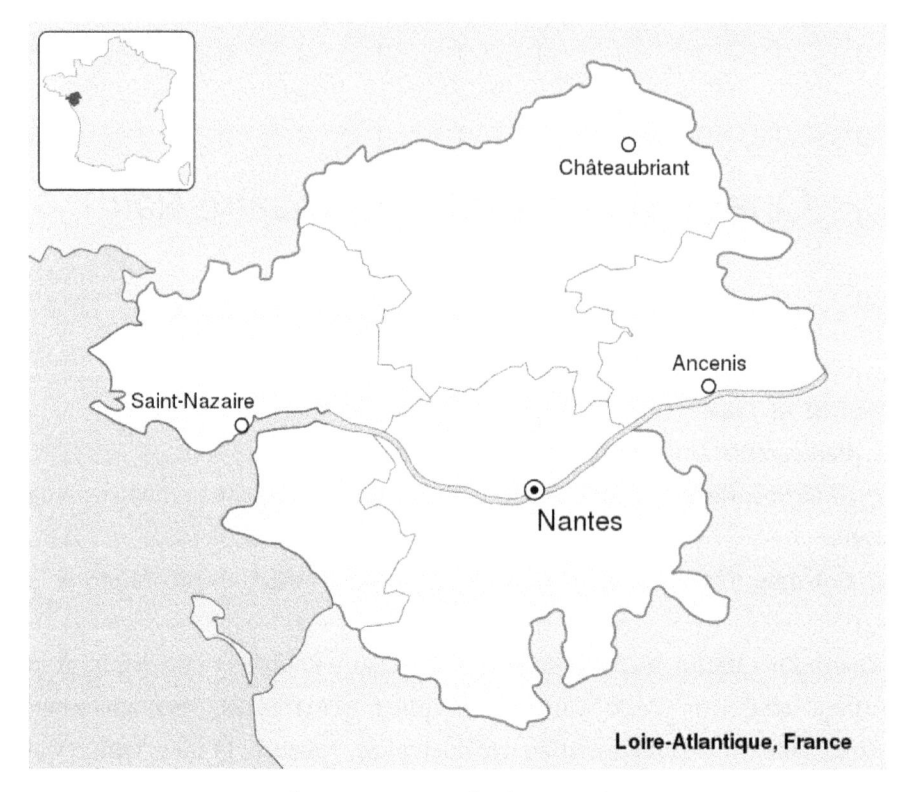

*Figure 25.* Map of Saint Nazaire.

## Background

St.Nazaire is a town in western France with a major harbor on the right bank of the Loire estuary, near the Atlantic Ocean. It had gates that could control the water level so the tide did not affect it. When the Germans conquered France, they converted the port to a major dry dock and repair station.

The raid aimed to destroy the gates, water pumping machinery, and shipping in the area. This would deny the use of this dry dock to the German Navy, thus limiting their ability to repair and refit their capital ships and submarines. A particular target was the Tirpitz, sister ship of the Bismarck.

The operation involved a daring and complex plan that included a combined force of Royal Navy and Commandos. The RAF also planned diversionary attacks. It originally involved using an old French destroyer accompanied by Free French forces, but the admiralty later dismissed this plan as they felt too many people would know the plan.

## Operation

Under the command of Commander Robert Ryder, the raiding force comprised the destroyer HMS Campbeltown, which was specially modified to resemble a German vessel, along with several motor launches and smaller craft carrying British Commandos. The Campbeltown was loaded with explosives and designed to ram the dry dock gates.

The raiding force successfully reached St. Nazaire, with the Campbeltown crashing into the dry dock's outer gates, leaving a 30-foot gash on the ship. Commandos rushed out of the damaged ship, destroying 2 winding stations and an underground pumping station, causing significant damage. Although the mission was a success, most of the motor launches that should've taken the commandos back to safety had been destroyed. This resulted in the capture of many raiders.

**Figure 26.** The British destroyer HMS Campbeltown blocking the dry dock.

## Aftermath

At first the Germans thought that the damage was minimal and could easily be repaired, but at noon the following day, the Campbeltown exploded, killing at least two captured commandos who were brought back to the ship for interrogation. This explosion rendered the docks unusable.

The dry dock remained unusable for the rest of the war, disrupting German naval operations. They only repaired it in 1947.

Operation Chariot was a remarkable example of audacity, bravery, and precision planning. It remains one of the most celebrated and daring British commando raids of World War II. The raid demonstrated the effectiveness of Special Forces operations and their ability to strike at key enemy infrastructure.

It also increased German paranoia, as they feared no ports or shore facilities were safe from sabotage.

# Operation Anthropoid (Assassination of Reinhard Heydrich, the Butcher of Prague)

*May 27, 1942*

**Belligerents:** Czechoslovakia with support from the United Kingdom vs. Germany

**Objective:** Assassinate top-ranking Nazi general Reinhard Heydrich, also known as the "Butcher of Prague"

**Outcome:** Heydrich successfully assassinated, resulting in brutal reprisals against the perpetrators and the nearby civilian population.

## Background

Operation Anthropoid was the codename for a Czechoslovak military operation during World War II. It was the only successful government-organized assassination of a top-ranking Nazi official.

It was a mission undertaken by Czechoslovak soldiers in exile with the goal of assassinating Reinhard Heydrich, a high-ranking Nazi official.

Heydrich, known as the "Butcher of Prague," was the Reich Protector of Bohemia and Moravia, a territory that encompassed the present-day Czech Republic. He was a key figure in the Nazi regime and infamous for his brutality. In January 1942 he presided over the Wannsee Conference where they planned the implementation of the Final Solution, the systematic extermination of European Jews.

## Operation

Operation Anthropoid was carried out on May 27, 1942, in Prague, Czechoslovakia. Ján Kubiš and Jozef Gabčík, two Czechoslovak soldiers trained by the British Special Operations Executive (SOE), led the mission. The operatives parachuted into Czechoslovakia and contacted the local resistance.

The plan involved ambushing Heydrich's car as he traveled through the city and launching a direct attack on him. During the operation, Gabčík attempted to assassinate Heydrich with a Sten submachine gun, but the weapon malfunctioned. Kubiš then threw a modified anti-tank grenade at Heydrich's vehicle, severely injuring him.

Heydrich survived the attack, but he later succumbed to his injuries on June 4, 1942.

*Figure 27.* Reinhard Heydrich's car (a Mercedes-Benz 320 Convertible B) after the assassination attempt in Prague. Heydrich later died of his injuries.

## Aftermath

In retaliation, the Nazis launched a brutal crackdown on the Czech population, including the murder of over 5,000 civilians and the complete destruction of the village of Lidice. The Germans also destroyed Ležáky, another village after equipment from the assassins was found there.

The Germans finally caught the assassins at the Cathedral of Sts Cyril and Methodius. They were killed along with the Bishop and priests of the church.

With Heydrich's death, planning and implementation of the Final Solution fell upon his subordinate, Adolph Eichmann.

***Figure 28.*** The crypt where the Czech soldiers hid and later made their last stand.

# Operation MI (Battle of Midway, 1942)

*June 4 to 7, 1942*

**Belligerents:** Japan vs. the United States

**Objectives:** Seize Midway Island and force the US Navy in a decisive battle and destroy it.

**Outcome:** Amphibious landing canceled. Disastrous Japanese defeat as they lose all four fleet carriers.

Operation MI was a major offensive undertaken by the Imperial Japanese Navy to capture Midway Atoll and eliminate the remaining American aircraft carriers in the Pacific.

Under Operation MI, the Japanese devised an intricate plan to draw out and destroy the American carriers. The plan involved a diversionary attack on the Aleutian Islands, specifically the islands of Attu and Kiska, to mislead the Americans into believing that the main Japanese intended to invade there. This diversion aimed to draw American forces away from Midway and weaken their defenses.

Simultaneously, the main Japanese fleet, including four large aircraft carriers (Akagi, Kaga, Sōryū, and Hiryū), planned to launch an assault on Midway Island itself. The aim was to neutralize the American base, secure the atoll, and engage and destroy any American carriers that responded to the threat.

**Figure 29.** The aircraft carrier Akagi, flagship at Midway of the of the Imperial Japanese Navy's Kidō Butai.

## Background

By April 1942, the empire of Japan was at the peak of its powers. They had taken Hong Kong, British Malaya, Singapore, the Dutch East Indies and most of the Philippines. They were confident and felt secure. But on April 18, 1942, the Americans launched the Doolittle Raid and bombed Tokyo. Although the damage was relatively minimal, the raid's impact shook the Japanese military establishment, revealing the capability of aircraft carriers to strike Japan's home islands. This realization united the usually divided Japanese military behind Admiral Isoroku Yamamoto's leadership, as they recognized the urgent need to neutralize the American carriers. Yamamoto aimed for a definitive naval confrontation to eliminate the American carriers from the Pacific theater.

A few months before the battle, there were four American carriers—the

Enterprise, Yorktown, Lexington, and Hornet. Yamamoto knew that the Kido Butai, the world's most advanced naval aviation force, was capable of destroying them all.

And even before Midway, Yamamoto believed he had a stroke of luck. In May 1942, the two navies fought the Battle of the Coral Sea. A Japanese carrier was heavily damaged, but they believed that they had sunk two of the American carriers, the Lexington and the Yorktown, leaving the Americans with just two carriers.

Yamamoto liked his chances.

*Figure 30.* The Battle of the Coral Sea on May 8, 1942. A mushroom cloud rises after a heavy explosion on board the U.S. Navy aircraft carrier USS Lexington (CV-2). In this battle, the Japanese thought they sank both the Lexington and the Yorktown.

## Operation

Unknown to the Japanese, the Yorktown survived the battle and limped back to Pearl Harbor. But the Japanese continued assuming it had been sunk and continued to plan their attack against just two carriers.

Yamamoto's plan was complex. First the four fleet carriers under Vice-Admiral Nagumo would attack Midway's defenses to soften them up. The Japanese would then seize Kure Island, an atoll near Midway and seaplane base. Finally, an amphibious landing force would seize Midway and neighboring atolls.

Yamamoto was convinced that the Americans were not expecting an attack, and by the time the main battle fleet from Hawaii reacted, the Japanese should've constructed a strong defense. He would use the four carriers and the island itself as an unsinkable fifth carrier.

The Japanese admiral had three sets of forces designed to destroy the US carriers.

1. A fleet of submarines guarded the area around Pearl Harbor. Once the carrier force left the port, this submarine group would harass this force.
2. Aircraft from the carriers and Midway Island itself will attack those that survived the submarines.
3. Finally, those that survive the air attack will have to contend with battleships and cruisers, including the Yamato—the biggest battleship ever built.

### *Target AF*

What Yamamoto didn't know was that a month before he even set sail, the Americans already knew his plans. They had broken parts of the Japanese code, giving US Commander Joseph Rochefort and his intelligence team an idea of the force sailing towards them. They had a rough estimate of the size of the force, approximate location, and likely target code-named AF.

Rochefort's superiors in Washington were not convinced that AF was Midway. To prove this, he sent a message to the base at Midway via an underground cable. He asked them to send a message that they were having problems with their water purification system having broken down. Shortly after, they intercepted a Japanese message saying that AF had water problems. This proved that Yamamoto's target was Midway.

SCHEMES

*Figure 31.* Aerial photograph of Midway Atoll. Midway's airfield on Eastern Island is in the foreground.

## *American Deployment*

On May 28, the American fleet left Pearl Harbor and assembled at a point called Point Luck. The carriers Hornet and Enterprise were joined by the Yorktown, which was being patched up even as she prepared for battle.

And by the time the Japanese submarine force arrived at Pearl Harbor, the carrier task force had already left port and was now hundreds of miles away.

*Figure 32.* The U.S. Navy aircraft carrier USS Enterprise (CV-6), the most decorated American warship in World War 2. Photo taken in between the Battles of the Coral Sea and Midway.

## Search

Even though the Americans had radar, they still sent a huge reconnaissance force, composed mainly of 31 PBY Catalinas and TBF Avengers. As a result, as early as June 3, the Catalinas had detected the amphibious landing force. Later, Catalinas also found parts of the main Japanese carrier group.

In contrast, it is said that despite having no effective radar, Nagumo sent less than 10 scout planes. The Japanese simply did not expect to find anything waiting for them. They were waiting to confirm a negative.

### *Initial Attacks*

Once the US confirmed the location of the Japanese fleet, planes from Midway Island launched. The bombers proceeded to the carrier force while the fighters stayed behind to protect the island. Majority of the American fighter planes were Brewster F2A Buffalos, which were obsolete and were no match against the Zeros. Several Wildcats complemented the air defense.

The bombers on the hand were a mix of old and new dive bombers, B-17 flying fortresses, and B-26 Marauders. When they attacked, they failed to do much damage. The closest their attack came to success was when a damaged B-26 tried to crash on the Japanese carrier Akagi. It was close, but missed.

OPERATION MI (BATTLE OF MIDWAY, 1942)

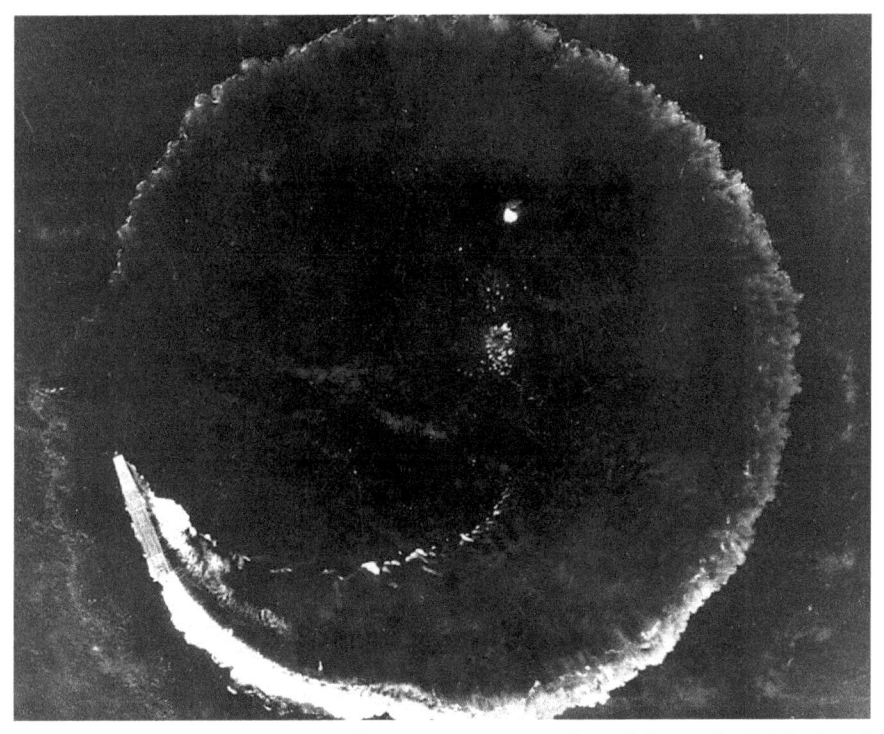

*Figure 33*. The Japanese aircraft carrier Soryu circles while under high-level bombing attack by USAAF B-17 bombers from the Midway base. This attack produced near misses, but no hits.

Although they faced intense anti-aircraft fire, the Japanese attackers had better success, as they mauled the mostly obsolete fighters. And when there were no more targets in the air, the zeroes strafed the island even as the runways were empty of planes. But at 7 am, the leader of the Japanese radioed that a second attack was needed. They hadn't disabled the runways and the defensive weapons that could attack the landing forces.

### Nagumo's dilemma

Once a scout plane confirmed the presence of an American fleet about 200 miles away from him, Japanese plans went awry. Nagumo was shaken. Why were the carriers in the area instead of at Pearl Harbor? Worse, was it possible that the Americans had already launched an attack? But launching an attack of their own was complicated. The first wave of planes that had attacked Midway was on their way back. And his fighter screen was running out of fuel. Worse, many of his current planes had anti-ground, not anti-ship weapons.

Nagumo had to make a decision. Should he let the first wave and the fighters hover above the fleet and send out 36 Val Dive-bombers to attack the Americans? This meant he would attack with limited or no support from torpedo planes and zeros.

Or should he recover the planes and then launch a full-scale attack as dictated by Japanese naval doctrine?

From the carrier Hiryū, Rear Admiral Yamaguchi Tamon, who also received the scouting report, sent Nagumo unsolicited advice by blinker signal. "Consider it advisable to launch attack force immediately."

Nagumo ignored him and decided on the second option. He'd recover all his planes, rearm them with the right weapons and hit the US carriers with a coordinated, full strike. This was in accordance with Japanese naval doctrine — attack with the biggest force you can muster. This was the most fateful decision in the battle.

### *Torpedo and Dive Bombers Arrive*

As Nagumo's fleet prepared for a coordinated attack, American torpedo planes arrived in several batches. The carriers maneuvered to avoid them, further hampering recovery and launch of airplanes. More significantly, the fighter cover also flew lower to engage the slow, lumbering torpedo planes. And even though destroyed almost all torpedo planes, they were running out of ammunition.

Once the threat from the torpedo planes subsided, Nagumo was prepared to launch his strike force. At that precise moment, however, dive-bombers arrived from different directions. And high above the clouds, there were no zero fighters to harass them, giving them a direct approach to the carriers.

In the next five minutes, three of the four Japanese carriers would be burning wrecks. Kaga and Sōryū were each hit with at least three bombs.

The flagship Akagi suffered only one hit, but it penetrated the hangar deck and exploded amidst the fueled aircraft with anti-ship weapons, as well as the anti-land bombs pushed to the side.

### *Hiryū counter attacks*

The Hiryū was also attacked, but it suffered no damage. As the sole surviving carrier, it launched an attack that set the Yorktown ablaze.

For a moment this gave Nagumo hope, as he believed that it's likely the Hiryū is facing just one other American carrier. Hours later, planes from the Hiryū attacked once more. As they did earlier, the carrier was ablaze. Confident that they had sunk two carriers, the pilots returned to Hiryū to rest briefly and eat. What they didn't know was they had attacked Yorktown a second time. Yorktown's damage control team had erased signs of damages from the first attack —containing flames and repairing the deck.

Soon, the US launched a massive attack composed mainly of dive-bombers. And Hiryū, the last remaining carrier, finally sank.

***Figure 34.*** The US aircraft carrier Yorktown (CV-5) burning after the first attack by Japanese bombers from the Hiryu.

*Figure 35.* U.S. Navy Douglas SBD-3 Dauntless dive bombers from the aircraft carrier USS Hornet (CV-8) approaching the burning Japanese heavy cruiser Mikuma to make the third set of attacks on her, during the Battle of Midway, 6 June 1942.

## Aftermath

The Battle of Midway is widely regarded as a turning point in the Pacific War, as it not only halted the Japanese advance but also marked the first major defeat for Japan's carrier fleet. It also meant that from that point onward, Japan wouldn't have air superiority when they launched amphibious operations. This would have disastrous consequences in the New Guinea and Guadalcanal campaigns.

The battle shifted the balance of power in the Pacific and allowed the United

States to seize the initiative and begin an offensive against the Japanese in subsequent operations.

# Operation Jubilee (Raid at Dieppe)

*August 19, 1942*

*Belligerents:* Western Allies (mainly Canadians) vs. Germany

*Objectives:* Capture the port of Dieppe in northern France and hold it briefly. This will boost morale and convince the Soviet Union that the Western Allies were committed to a second front.

*Outcome:* An almost total Allied defeat.

## Background

Operation Jubilee, also known as the Dieppe Raid, was a major Allied amphibious assault on the German-occupied port of Dieppe in northern France during World War II. The operation took place on August 19, 1942, and was primarily conducted by Canadian, British, and American forces.

It has since been known as the dress rehearsal for Operation Overlord, which would happen in less than two years.

Operation Jubilee aimed to gather intelligence, test German defenses, and gain a foothold on the French coast. The Allies hoped to learn valuable lessons for future large-scale amphibious operations and divert German forces away from the Eastern Front.

The assault on Dieppe involved a combined landing force of just over 6,000 troops, supported by armor, and by the Royal Navy and Air Force. The plan included simultaneous landings on multiple beaches, with the focus on capturing and temporarily holding key objectives in and around the town of Dieppe.

**Figure 36.** A submarine chaser laying a smoke screen during the Combined Operations daylight raid on Dieppe.

## Operation

Operation Jubilee encountered significant difficulties from the outset. The Allies lost the element of surprise as spies had warned the Germans about the attack. The invasion fleet also had the misfortune of encountering a small German convoy on the way to the landing. On the beaches, the landing forces faced strong German resistance, heavily fortified positions, and effective coastal defenses. The beaches were heavily mined, and the German forces were well prepared and waiting.

The operation involved landing in six beaches in Dieppe, codenamed Blue,

Green, Orange, Red, White, and Yellow.

### Blue Beach

The delay in the landing meant that the smokescreen intended to cover the landing forces' movement had lifted. The 556-man Royal Regiment of Canada was almost completely destroyed as a fighting force. 200 were killed and 264 were captured.

### Green Beach

The Canadians originally landed undetected, but much of the group landed in the wrong area. As they advanced, a German force had beaten them to the only bridge leading them to their aim, the hills east of their landing area. They were forced to retreat as the Germans prepared to counterattack in force.

### Orange Beach

The group's mission was to neutralize the coastal battery Hess that had six 150 mm guns. The commando unit composed of British soldiers and US Army Rangers successfully achieved its mission.

### Red Beach

Located on the east end of Dieppe, the Essex Scottish regiment landed here and were trapped by the seawall. Churchill tanks were supposed to land with the troops, but these arrived late. 29 tanks landed, but only 15 made it across the seawall where anti-tank obstacles ultimately stopped them.

### White Beach

Located on the west end of Dieppe, the Royal Hamilton Division landed here. This was adjacent to the Red Beach and was also subjected to the same carnage and difficulties.

### Yellow Beach

The commando's mission was to silence the coastal battery near Bernevall, which had three 170 mm and four 105 mm guns. They failed to destroy the guns and were forced to withdraw.

**Figure 37.** German soldiers examining a Calgary Regiment "Churchill" tank abandoned during the raid on Dieppe

## Aftermath

The Germans had enough advanced knowledge about the raid and prepared for the landing. It didn't help that the naval bombardment was insufficient to soften the defenses.

Despite the soldiers' individual bravery and heroism, the raid was a disaster for the Allies. Within the day, over half of the forces who landed were killed, missing, or captured. It was a costly failure for the Allies.

The operation highlighted the challenges of conducting amphibious landings against well-prepared enemy defenses and provided valuable lessons for subsequent successful operations, such as the D-Day landings. Most importantly, it highlighted the need for operational secrecy.

This was also a propaganda coup for the Nazis, reinforcing their message that their empire was safe even if most of the military was fighting on the Eastern Front.

One of the captured leaders, General William Southam was even captured with the assault plan, allowing the Germans to study the operation. The faults in the plan probably added to the German hubris.

*Figure 38.* Commandos returning to Newhaven in their landing craft (LCAs).

After the raid, there were a variety of explanations on why the Allies conducted it—to boost morale and tell the Germans the Allies can attack France if they want to, thus diverting forces away from the Eastern front.

### *Was the Dieppe Raid an Elaborate Cover for Another Operation?*

In recent years, there have been claims that the raid at Dieppe was just a cover for a tiny operation—stealing German codes and Enigma machines.

Dieppe was a major German supply hub in the channel and contained sensitive communications equipment. So instead of a raid with specific intelligence gathering objectives, the Allied supposedly added multiple valuable and plausible objectives. Thus, if successful, the Germans wouldn't know that the real target was intelligence gathering.

Regardless of the true objective, it was an operation with a tragic loss of lives, mainly Canadian. The event was a monument to the courage and sacrifice of Canadians and other allied soldiers. It underscored the price that these soldiers paid on the way to victory.

# Operation Torch (Allied invasion of North Africa)

**November 8 to 16, 1942**

**Belligerents:** United States, United Kingdom, Canada, Australia, Netherlands, Free French vs. Vichy France, Germany, and Italy

**Objective:** Secure Morocco, Algeria, and French West Africa

**Outcome:** Allies capture objectives, but Germans react by launching Case Anton or the occupation of Vichy France by Germany and Italy

As the last days of the Second Battle of El Alamein raged on, the Allies landed in North Africa. The operation aimed to secure the North African coastline, gain control of key ports and draw Axis forces away from the Eastern Front, relieving the Soviet Union.

It was also a compromise operation. The landings gave the British a chance to secure victory in North Africa and at the same time allowed the Americans the chance to fight against the Nazis on a limited scale. Although the Americans had been fighting bloody battles in the Pacific, this was their first major involvement in the European-North African theater.

This was Operation Torch.

## Background

In late 1942 French North Africa was still nominally under the Vichy regime. As the British finally got the upper hand vs. the Afrika Korps, the Allies hoped that a landing in North Africa would trigger a pincer attack and finally drive the Axis from the continent.

The Allies expected the Vichy French Army defending the coast to defect to their side. As long-time allies, they believed the French land forces would put up nothing more than a token resistance. The navy had reservations, though. Months earlier, as part of Operation Catapult, the English fleet attacked the French Navy and killed 1,300 French sailors and officers. It was likely they had to overcome some animosity. The key was getting French Admiral Francois Darlan on their side.

Under the command of General Dwight D. Eisenhower, a combined force of American, British, and other Allied troops landed in three primary locations: Casablanca, Oran, and Algiers. The landing forces faced varying degrees of resistance from Vichy French forces, who initially supported the Axis powers but later switched allegiance to the Allies during the operation.

Despite initial difficulties and confusion, the Allied forces achieved their objectives. They secured control of the major ports, neutralized or persuaded Vichy French forces to join the Allied cause, and established a foothold in North Africa. The success of Operation Torch set the stage for further Allied advances in the Mediterranean, including the subsequent campaigns in Sicily and mainland Italy.

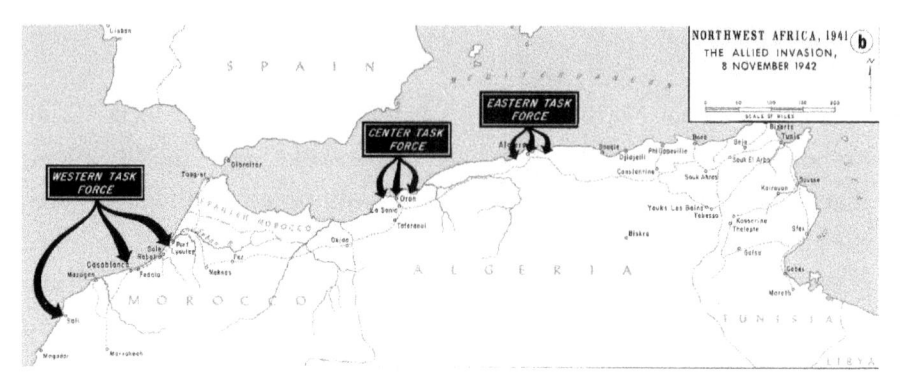

Figure 39. Allied landing sites during Operation Torch.

## Operation

With the attack on Mers El Kébir still fresh in everyone's minds, the Allies were careful to frame this as an American operation, with the British only supporting them.

The Americans planned to land on Morocco's Atlantic coast (Safi, Fedala, and Mehdiya-Port Lyautey), with Casablanca as the primary goal. Simultaneously, a combined Anglo-American army would land on Algeria's Mediterranean coast targeting Oran and Algiers. An airborne assault near Oran complemented the landings to seize two airports.

Since the Allies expected little to no resistance from the French, there were no preliminary bombardments. However, the initially stiff French defenses caused heavy losses among the landing forces. Complicating the political scene, a failed coup attempt by pro-Allied French General Antoine Béthouart also alerted the Vichy French about the invasion.

## OPERATION TORCH (ALLIED INVASION OF NORTH AFRICA)

*Figure 40.* Troops landing near Algiers. They're carrying a large American flag (left side) hoping that the French Army wouldn't fire on them.

The Allies encountered varying degrees of success during the landings. The most challenging operation took place in Fedala, where adverse weather conditions disrupted the landings, and a French naval sortie added further difficulties. In Oran, the Allies aimed to capture ships and port facilities, but the Vichy French thwarted their plans, resulting in the destruction of targeted assets. Additionally, the airborne landing in Oran was scattered and played a minimal role in the city's capture.

In contrast, the landing at Algiers proceeded smoothly, as French resistance staged a coup and neutralized all coastal batteries, facilitating the Allies' progress. By November 10, the Allied forces had achieved all their landing objectives, including the successful capture of Casablanca.

SCHEMES

*Figure 41.* The aircraft carrier USS Ranger (CV-4) off North Africa on 8 November 1942 for Operation Torch.

Despite facing significant challenges in some locations, the overall outcome of the landings proved to be successful, securing crucial strategic positions and gaining the cooperation of the Vichy French forces to support the Allied cause.

*Figure 42.* The landing ship Karanja on fire after enemy attack in Bougie Harbour during the North African landings.

## Aftermath

Operation Torch had a massive military and political effect on the war.

French Admiral Francois Darlan ordered all French forces in North Africa to cooperate with the Allies. In return, they made him French "High Commissioner" in North Africa to the chagrin of Charles de Gaulle. The French Expeditionary Corps, composed of forces from the region, then took part in the Italian campaign, gaining recognition for being among the first units to breach Germany's formidable Gustav line, a critical defensive barrier.

In response to the French's defection to the Allies, Hitler occupied Southern France. They also tried to seize the French naval assets. This resulted in the scuttling of the major French fleet at Toulon on November 27.

Operation Torch was a significant turning point in the war. It marked the beginning of the end for Axis control in North Africa and paved the way for the eventual Allied invasion of Italy.

# Operation Uranus (Soviet Counterattack in Stalingrad)

*November 19 to 23, 1942*

   *Belligerents:* Soviet Union vs. Germany and its Allies
   *Objective:* Destroy the Axis forces in and around Stalingrad
   *Outcome:* Relief of Stalingrad. Encirclement of the Axis forces including the German Sixth Army.

Operation Uranus, also known as the Battle of Stalingrad Strategic Offensive, was a major Soviet military operation during World War II. It was launched on November 19, 1942, with the aim of encircling and destroying the German 6th Army and other Axis forces fighting in the vicinity of Stalingrad.

   The Soviet High Command meticulously planned the operation, taking advantage of the weakly defended flanks of the German forces. While the depleted German Sixth Army was still formidable, the Romanians manning the flanks were under-equipped and relatively inexperienced.

   Under Operation Uranus, the Soviets deployed a significant force comprising multiple armies, totaling over a million soldiers. The offensive involved coordinated attacks from the north and south, aimed at linking up and encircling the German forces in a massive pincer movement.

## Background

Amidst the fierce battle of Stalingrad, the war of attrition between Germany and the Soviet Union intensified, unleashing brutal confrontations. Despite Nazi propaganda claiming victory, the Russians tenaciously still held about 10% of the city and were reinforced by limited supplies and troops arriving from the Volga. The Germans had even worse supply issues, but they believed that the Russians were on the verge of collapse. Greatly outnumbering the 47,000 Soviets in the city, they launched Operation Hubertus, believing a final, decisive push would swiftly crush the Soviet pockets of resistance.

*Figure 43.* Soviet tanks advance in the snowy steppe during Operation Uranus.

They were so confident that Kurt Zeisler, German Chief of Staff also declared that the Soviet Union was incapable of launching any major attacks on the Eastern front. But Operation Hubertus failed.

## Operation

On November 19, with the weather at -25 degrees Celsius, to the Nazis' surprise and bewilderment, the Soviets launched a counterattack. The 80-minute artillery bombardment from mortars, guns, and Katyusha rocket-launchers hit the German flanks in a 20-kilometer front. This was followed by an attack by half a million Soviet infantry and armor. The Romanians manning the flanks held initial assaults, but the lack of anti-tank artillery and weapons proved fatal as the Russians ultimately broke through. By the end of the day, the Romanians were on the run.

An artillery barrage on the other German flank soon followed this with an artillery barrage. After this bombardment armor and infantry from Beketovka attacked.

The German defended fiercely and were reinforced by their only reserve, the 29th Panzergrenadier Division, but the collapse of the Romanian flank proved critical. By November 20, the Soviets had ripped a hole in the flanks of the German 4th Panzer.

A day later, two Soviet armies were 30 kilometers in the German rear, placing the Nazis in real danger of encirclement. By the 23rd, Stalingrad was surrounded.

**Figure 44.** Soviet troops advance on Kalach during Operation Uranus.

Worse for the Germans, the Soviets had also formed an outer defensive ring to block reinforcements.

## Aftermath

About 300,000 soldiers were trapped in the encircled city. They prepared to break out only to get Hitler's order to stay put. Hitler believed he could resupply the city by air and a rescue Army could still link up with them.

But the Luftwaffe failed to deliver enough supplies and a relief force led by Erich von Manstein was stopped. Despite Manstein's pleas to let the Sixth Army break up and possibly link up with his force, Hitler refused. The Sixth Army was on its own.

Just over two months later, Friedrich Paulus became the first German Field Marshal to surrender. His decimated army of over 120,000 starving and frostbitten men could fight no more.

Operation Uranus was a crucial Soviet success that had significant strategic and psychological effects on the course of the war. It not only halted the German advance but also set the stage for the subsequent Soviet offensives that pushed the German forces back and ultimately led to the liberation of the Soviet Union and the defeat of Nazi Germany.

# Operation I-Go (Japanese Counterattack in the Solomons and New Guinea)

**April 1 to 16, 1943**

**Belligerents:** Japan vs. the United States

**Objectives:** Launch an aerial attack on US forces in the Solomons and New Guinea and buy time for the Japanese to strengthen perimeter defenses.

**Outcome:** A stalemate, though the Japanese believed they won a major victory

Operation I-Go was a Japanese attempt to seize the initiative in the Pacific in 1943. The Japanese Imperial Forces planned to launch air attacks on Allied forces and installations in the Solomons and New Guinea. They hoped it would stop the Allies' island-hopping operations and allow the Japanese time to construct a stronger defensive perimeter.

It was the last offensive planned by Admiral Isoroku Yamamoto. Just two days after the operation ended, he flew to the area to personally congratulate frontline troops in I-Go. P38 Lightning fighters attacked his air convoy and shot down his plane.

*Figure 45.* IJN commander Admiral Isoroku Yamamoto (left) with Admiral Jinichi Kusaka (center) at Rabaul in April 1943, shortly before Yamamoto's death.

## Background

In 1943, the Japanese knew they had to strengthen their defensive perimeter. To reinforce their bases at Lae and Salamaua in March 1943, they attempted to send reinforcements to these bases. Instead, the Allies intercepted the convoy, resulting in the loss of 12 ships and almost 3,000 men. This proved how dominant Allied air power was in the theater.

Unless they could somehow slow down the Allies and build a stronger defense, their forward bases would fall one by one.

## Operation

To counter the US' recent victories and aggressive offensive, Admiral Yamamoto devised a plan to launch a series of air attacks on major Allied bases. A major concern, however, was the lack of experienced pilots. While Japanese manufacturing maintained a fairly constant production of planes, Japan couldn't easily replace its roster of experienced pilots.

Yamamoto was aware of this and to mitigate the risk, he complemented the land-based aircraft with those of the experienced and highly-trained Japanese Third Fleet, including from the carriers Zuikaku, Zuiho, Junyo, and Hiyo. As a result, Yamamoto had over 350 planes for the operation.

In the next few days, the Japanese attacked Guadalcanal, Buna, Port Moresby, and Milne Bay. Results were modest except for Milne Bay where the Allies had rerouted their ships following the attack on Port Moresby. The attack by 196 planes, most of which came from the carrier group, seriously damaged the anchorage and damaged a troop transport, a cargo ship, and minesweepers.

*Figure 46.* Japanese aircraft for Operation I-Go at Rabaul

While the raids inflicted actual damage, Japanese pilots exaggerated their reports up to five or six times. This was true for the other raids as well, leading Tokyo to believe the offensive was a massive success. The pilots also claimed to have destroyed 175 aircraft and sank 28 ships. Many of the ships only suffered minor damage, and they were immediately repaired. In reality, the Japanese sank a destroyer, a tanker, 2 transports, and a corvette, along with destroying 25 aircraft including several on land. For this victory, the Japanese paid the price with 55 lost aircraft.

The apparent victory led Yamamoto to personally congratulate the frontline troops, leading to his fateful trip.

## Aftermath

Radar and the Allied intelligence's ability to read Japanese messages prevented the operation from being a massive success. In every attack, the Allies could scramble fighters on time to defend the targets. Nevertheless, the overwhelming number of Japanese planes, the most since Pearl Harbor, was able to damage Allied facilities. It also had the result of the US putting many of their fighters on reserve to counter future Japanese attacks.

In the end, this operation resulted in US' offensive actions being delayed by only about 10 days. Worst of all, the Japanese soon lost Yamamoto, their most capable naval strategist.

# Operation Mincemeat (Deception Campaign for the Invasion of Sicily)

*April 1943*

   *Belligerents:* United Kingdom vs. Germany (British Intelligence vs. the Abwehr)

   *Objective:* Make the Germans believe the Allies were landing elsewhere, not Sicily

   *Outcome:* Near total success as the Nazis sent reinforcements to the Balkans.

Operation Mincemeat was a World War II deception plan carried out by the British intelligence agency, MI5, in 1943. The aim of the operation was to deceive the Axis powers, particularly Germany, about the Allied invasion plans for Sicily.

## Background

Following the triumph in North Africa, military strategists shifted their focus to the next objective. France remained the ultimate goal, but it remained unfeasible. As alternatives, attention turned to two options: Sicily and Greece or the Balkans.

   During the Casablanca conference, the Allies made a strategic decision to focus on Sicily, codenamed Operation Husky. Recognizing the need for deception, they devised Operation Mincemeat as part of Operation Barclay, aiming to mislead the Germans into believing the landings would take place in Greece or the Balkans. By employing this clever ruse, the Allies aimed to gain a tactical advantage in their preparations for the Sicilian campaign.

## Operation

British intelligence decided they needed to send a fake dead soldier who had sufficient, credible information about the impending invasion. They expected the enemy to seize the body and find a briefcase with letters and documents about an invasion of the Balkans.

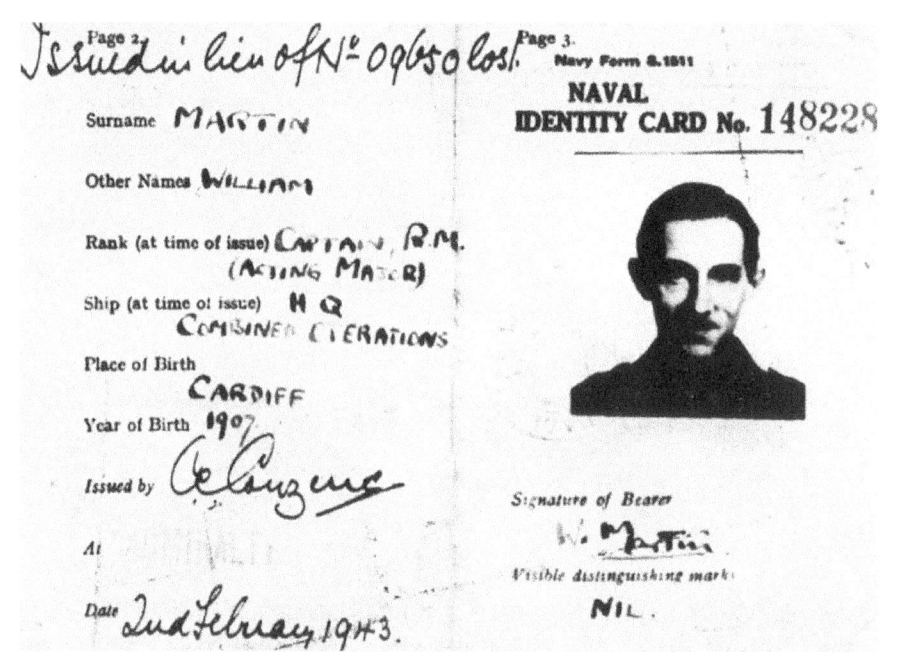

**Figure 47.** Naval identity card of the fictitious British Major Martin.

They gave the corpse a new identity—Major William Martin of the Royal

Marines. They chose the name because the British military had men with the same name and similar ranks. The rank also meant that it was high enough for him to be trusted with sensitive information, but low enough not to be instantly recognized by everybody. To complete the ruse, they placed love letters and a receipt for a diamond engagement ring.

But most importantly, among the documents found with him are the correspondence between two British generals that suggested that Sicily was just a feint and that the actual target was Greece and Sardinia.

A submarine delivered the body of the fake Major Martin to Spain, which was nominally neutral but collaborated with the Germans in World War 2. The planners hoped that the predominantly Catholic Spaniards would be averse to performing extensive post-mortem examinations. They also expected the Spanish to share their find with the Germans. To confirm this, they placed a single eyelash in the letter. The eyelash would move or disappear if the letter were opened.

**Figure 48.** The submarine HMS Seraph. Seraph launched the body of "Major Martin" near the Spanish coast.

The body was found by a local fisherman and then taken to Huelva by the Spanish authorities. The British vice-consul in the city was informed, and he immediately informed England. At that time, British intelligence knew the Germans could read the vice-consul's messages, and they responded that the briefcase had sensitive information and they should recover it immediately.

The body was buried with full military honors while the briefcase was returned to the vice-consul. British intelligence later discovered that the eyelash in the letter was missing, indicating it was opened. To complete the ruse, British intelligence told the vice-consul that they had examined the letters and they were not opened. The Germans also captured this message.

A few days later Bletchley Park intercepted a message from the Germans saying that the invasion was in the Balkans. This was the conclusive proof the British had that Operation Mincemeat was a success.

## Aftermath

Mussolini believed Sicily was the Allies' next target, but Hitler ignored him, partly because of information from Operation Mincemeat, and partly because Mussolini's army had been losing badly.

The German forces' strategic response to the Allies' plans was significant, as they relocated the experienced 1st Panzer Division to Greece, bolstered their fighter aircraft and torpedo boats, and doubled troop strength at Sardinia. Despite these challenges, the Allies managed to accomplish their operation in just 38 days, a remarkable feat compared to the initial expectation of 90 days. Operation Mincemeat, with its ingenious and highly effective deception tactics, remains one of the most remarkable and pivotal operations of the war.

# Operation Vengeance (The Plot to Kill Admiral Yamamoto)

*April 18, 1943*

*Belligerents:* United States vs. Japan
*Objective:* Assassinate Japanese Admiral Isoroku Yamamoto
*Outcome:* Yamamoto killed in the air over Bougainville Island

Operation Vengeance was the plan to assassinate Admiral Isoroku Yamamoto, the mastermind behind the attack on Pearl Harbor and the Commander-in-Chief of the Japanese Combined Fleet. While personally overseeing Operation I-Go in Rabaul, Yamamoto made the fateful decision to visit the frontline troops, unwittingly revealing his itinerary through decoded Japanese messages. US intelligence knew of his punctuality and strict adherence to discipline, making it likely that he would arrive precisely as planned.

The operation's name, "Vengeance," paid homage to Yamamoto's pivotal role in the attack on Pearl Harbor and represented the Americans' thirst for retribution. As one of the most prominent figures in the Japanese military, the opportunity to eliminate him was too tempting to ignore. His assassination left an irreplaceable void in their ranks, highlighting the significant impact of his loss.

# OPERATION VENGEANCE (THE PLOT TO KILL ADMIRAL YAMAMOTO)

*Figure 49.* The last photograph of Admiral Yamamoto, taken shortly before his plane was shot down.

## Background

Morale of the Japanese Army and Navy in the Solomons was low in March 1943. The long battles, huge casualties, and eventual evacuation from the Guadalcanal and New Guinea campaigns cast a dark shadow on the military's spirits. They also suffered a disaster at the Battle of the Bismarck Sea where they lost almost 3,000 experienced troops while in transport.

To seize the initiative and stop the Allied onslaught, Yamamoto went to Rabaul and launched Operation I-Go, a counter-offensive in the Solomons and New Guinea. It was a series of air attacks designed to halt the US island-hopping campaign and allow the Japanese to construct a better defensive perimeter.

Upon receiving the pilots' exaggerated reports, Yamamoto believed that I-Go was a success and wanted to congratulate the frontline troops.

## Operation

But the US code breakers knew his plans. They knew the date and time he would fly from Rabaul to Balalae Airfield on Bougainville. They also knew that they would come in on two Mitsubishi Betty bombers escorted by six Zero fighters.

As a result, the US Navy assembled a squadron of 18 P-38 Lightning fighters. Equipped with drop tanks, these planes were the only aircraft with the range to perform the mission and return to base. They would travel over 1,000 miles—the longest interception mission of World War 2.

**Figure 50.** The Lockheed P-38 Lightning, they type of airplane used by the pilots who shot down Yamamoto. At that was the only fighter capable of traveling over 1,000 miles

Yamamoto was expected to land at Balalae at 09:45 and the interception was set to 09:35. The interception team had to fly low to avoid radar and about 50 miles from shore to avoid observers. And because of the limited fuel, they only had about a 15-minute attack window.

They were split into two groups. A 4-plane group was designated "killer" or the ones to attack Yamamoto, while the rest formed the "cover" group, which will protect the attacking "killers."

When the raiders encountered Yamamoto's entourage, they wasted little time. The P-38s destroyed both Betty bombers. One disintegrated from a fuel tank hit while the other, containing Yamamoto, crashed into the jungle in flames.

When Yamamoto's body was recovered, he was still holding his unsheathed katana. A medical report identified two bullet wounds in Yamamoto's body. One in the shoulder and the fatal one in the head.

## Aftermath

When the pilots landed, there was no proper debriefing and controversies lingered on who actually shot down Yamamoto. Today, most historians credit Lt. Rex Barber with the kill.

**Figure 51.** Yamamoto's state funeral, June 5, 1943 — more than six weeks after his assassination.

For one month, the Japanese kept Yamamoto's death a secret. And when it was made public, the news of his death shocked Japan. Likewise, the Americans did not acknowledge the operation, partly because they didn't want the Japanese to suspect that they had broken their naval code. When presented with the news from the Japanese press, officials pretended to be surprised.

***Figure 52.*** Prime Minister Hideki Tojo bows to the funeral portrait of Admiral Isoroku Yamamoto in May 1943, after Yamamoto's remains were returned to Tokyo, Japan.

***Figure 53.*** Prime Minister Hideki Tojo bows to family members of Admiral Isoroku Yamamoto after Yamamoto's remains were returned to Japan.

With Yamamoto's death, a series of commanders took over his role—but none attained his stature, influence or success.

# Operation Chastise (The Dambusters Raid)

*May 16 to 17, 1943*

**Belligerents:** United Kingdom, Canada, and Australia vs. Germany

**Objective:** Destroy the hydroelectric dams in the Ruhr valley, Germany's industrial heartland

**Outcome:** Two major dams breached. Another two damaged but remained working. Forty percent casualty rate in the attack. Subsequent flooding killing over 1,000 Soviet POWs in the labor camps.

Operation Chastise, famously known as the Dambusters raid, was a daring and innovative air mission conducted by the Royal Air Force (RAF) during World War II. It took place on the night of May 16-17, 1943, and aimed to cripple the industrial heartland of Germany by targeting several key dams in the Ruhr Valley. Wing Commander Guy Gibson, of the newly formed No. 617 Squadron, led the operation. The airmen flew in specially modified Avro Lancaster bombers equipped with "bouncing bombs."

**Figure 54.** A reconnaissance photo of the Moehne Dam before the raid. The Moehne and Sorpe Dams supplied 75% of the water supplies for the Ruhr Valley industrial complex.

## Background

The Ruhr Valley was Germany's industrial heartland. Its dams provided hydroelectric power, pure water for steel making, and drinking water. It also controlled water levels in the existing canal transport system.

The Allies decided they should destroy the dams at Möhne, Eder, Sorpe, and

Ennepe. Aside from shutting down power, the subsequent flooding would also destroy or damage the factories nearby.

However, precision bombing was decades away and there were huge steel nets to protect the dam against torpedoes. They needed a different bomb. The solution was a "bouncing bomb" designed by Barnes Wallis. The bomb could skip over the water's surface and then detonate against the dam's wall, causing a breach. Delivering it required incredible skill as the planes had to drop the bombs at an altitude of just 60 feet to achieve skipping effect.

**Figure 55.** "Upkeep" bouncing bomb mounted under Wing Commander Gibson's Lancaster bomber.

Led by Wing Commander Guy Gibson, the newly formed No. 617 Squadron, equipped with specially modified Avro Lancaster bombers, embarked on the challenging mission. The Lancaster bombers carried an innovative bouncing bomb, designed by engineer Barnes Wallis that would skip over the water's surface before detonating against the dam walls. The low-altitude flight and precision required to breach the heavily fortified dams presented immense risks to the pilots. Nevertheless, the Dambusters successfully breached the Möhne and Eder dams, causing devastating floods and significant damage to German industry. The daring raid showcased the RAF's extraordinary capabilities and ingenuity during one of the most critical periods of World War II.

## Operation

There were three waves in the attack.

1. Wave One was split into three groups. The first group aimed for the Möhne dam. The second and third groups targeted the Eder dam.
2. Wave Two was to target the Sorpe and Ennepe dams.
3. Wave Three acted as backup to the first two. They took off two and a half hours later and would proceed to any dams that remained undamaged.

Executing the raid demanded flying at low altitudes to evade detection, leading to unfortunate accidents as a few planes inadvertently clipped power wires and crashed.

Approaching their designated targets necessitated flying at nearly level trajectories and releasing bombs from an exact height of 60 feet. The bombs were uniquely designed to induce a backspin of 500 rpm upon release.

Wing Commander Gibson was the first to drop his bomb and aimed for the Möhne dam. While it hit the target and exploded, it did not breach the dam. In subsequent attacks, he flew in front of the next bombers making the attack to draw flak to him and protect his comrades. His plane was damaged, but he survived the raid and was awarded the Victoria Cross.

Four bombs eventually hit Möhne dam, breaching it. They hit Eder dam with two bombs, also smashing it. Both Ennepe and Sorpe dams were hit but weren't breached.

*Figure 56.* Photograph of the breached Möhne Dam. Six Barrage balloons are above the dam

*Figure 57.* The breached Eder Dam.

## Aftermath

The raid inflicted significant damage on the Ruhr Valley. The breach of the Möhne and Eder dams caused devastating floods that disrupted transportation, flooded factories, and disrupted hydroelectric power generation. Operation returned to normal only four months after.

# OPERATION CHASTISE (THE DAMBUSTERS RAID)

*Figure 58.* A reconnaissance photo of the Ruhr Valley at Froendenberg-Boesperde, some 13 miles south from the Moehne Dam, showing massive flooding.

The Dambusters raid, while successful in breaching the dams and disrupting German industry, came at a significant cost. Of the 19 Lancaster bombers involved, eight were lost, resulting in the tragic loss of 53 airmen. Among the casualties, thirteen were Canadians, two were Australians, and the remainder served in the RAF.

Moreover, the subsequent floodings caused further loss of life, with over 1,600 individuals killed, many of them Soviet POWs assigned to labor camps. Despite the raid's achievements, the British missed the opportunity to fully capitalize on its impact. Albert Speer, the Nazi Armaments Minister, stated after the war that the British should have followed up with more conventional bombing to completely cripple the dams and their strategic significance.

The Dambusters raid, while a remarkable feat of bravery and ingenuity, served as a poignant reminder of the high price of war and the complexity of its outcomes.

# Operation Citadel (The Battle of Kursk)

*July 5 to July 17, 1943*

  *Belligerents:* Germany vs. the Soviet Union

  *Objectives*: Capture the Kursk salient, trap or destroy five Soviet armies, and return the strategic initiative to the Wehrmacht.

  *Outcome:* Germans failed to take Kursk. Soviets launch counteroffensive, Operations Kutuzov and Polkovodets Rumyantsev.

Operation Citadel, also known as the Battle of Kursk, was a major German offensive launched on the Eastern Front during World War II. The operation took place from July 5 to July 17, 1943, and it was the largest tank battle in history.

## Background

The objective of Operation Citadel was for the German forces, under the command of Field Marshal Erich von Manstein, to launch a powerful assault on the Kursk salient, a bulge in the Soviet lines near the city of Kursk in western Russia. The German High Command believed that a successful offensive at Kursk would cripple the Soviet defenses, leading to a breakthrough on the Eastern Front.

  Just a few months earlier, Von Manstein recovered the recently lost territories of Kharkiv and Belgorod. The Red Army fell back to Kursk and was likely saved by the spring mud season known as the rasputitsa. During this time, traveling on unpaved roads becomes difficult as they become muddy from rain or melting snow.

There was intense disagreement in the German high command on how to proceed. One group advocated adopting a mobile defensive position and then counterattack as weaknesses in the Red Army appear. Another pushed for an attack on Kursk, but it had to happen immediately.

Hitler agreed with the latter strategy, but critically delayed the attack for two months so the new Tiger and Panther tanks could take part in the battle. This proved to be a fatal mistake as it gave time to the Red Army to build stronger defenses.

The new tanks also strained the Wehrmacht's resources. They would deploy at least seven different tank /tank destroyer models ( Panzers II, III, and IV; Panther, Tiger, Wespe, and the Ferdinand). This, and the other armored vehicles made support and repair a nightmare. It didn't help that many of the units' productions were rushed resulting in breakdowns.

OPERATION CITADEL (THE BATTLE OF KURSK)

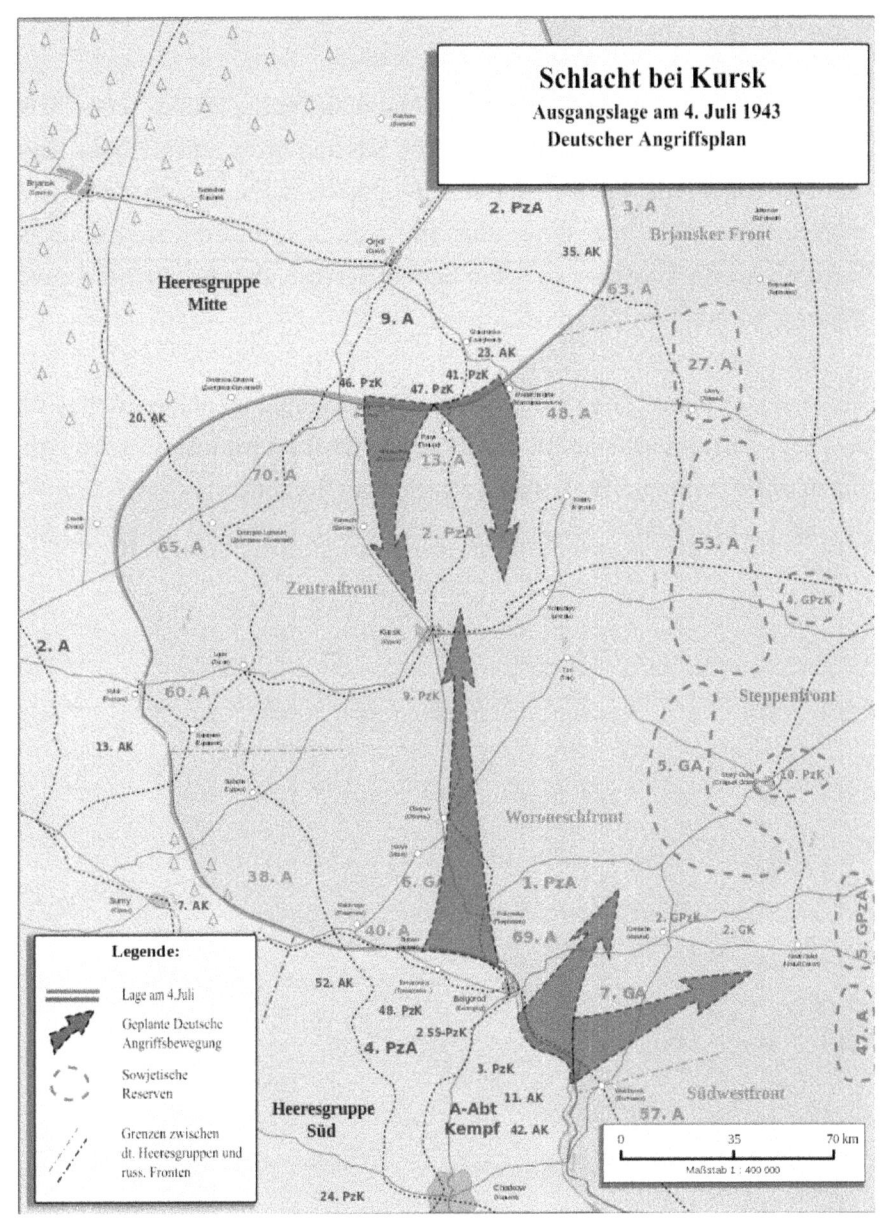

*Figure 59.* The German Plan and deployment of forces of both sides for the Battle of Kursk.

## Operation

Stalin initially wanted to attack, but Marshal Georgy Zhukov convinced him to go on the defensive instead. The Russian army and civilians from nearby villages built ditches, mines, anti-tank obstacles, and other defensive measures to whittle down the German strength. Once the Germans exhausted themselves attacking the two major lines of defense, they would then launch a counterattack. Stalin agreed.

The main German strategy involved double envelopment and encircling the five Soviet armies. General Walter Model's 9th Army would attack from the north while Hermann Hoth would attack from the south.

*Figure 60.* Panther tanks of 2nd SS Panzer Division Das Reich during Operation Citadel.

Hoth and von Manstein initiated the assault by attacking Oboyan, but their progress was hindered by heavy rain and muddy terrain. Worse, they also discovered that the Soviets strategically buried some T-34 tanks as anti-tank posts, negating the German advantage in range,

The German armies were able to penetrate the first lines of defense and the southern attack came close to overcoming the second line, but that was the closest they got to the Soviets' unfortified rear. The Germans couldn't overcome the Russian reserves, including the 5th Guards and 5th Guards Tank Army at Prokhorovka.

After four days of attacks, it was clear that Model didn't have enough forces to breach the Soviet lines, but they persevered to enable the southern thrust to break through. They fought for one more day, while the south fought for five more days until Hitler ordered von Manstein to stop.

*Figure 61.* A Panzer VI (Tiger I) during the Battle of Kursk.

Soviet losses were horrendous at more than triple the loss of the Germans, but the attacks had stalled. As the German numbers dwindled, the Soviets continued using reserves to plug gaps. Eventually the Germans had to withdraw, paving the way for the Soviet counterattacks.

*Figure 62.* A company of American-supplied M3 Lee Lend-Lease tanks advances to the frontline of the 6th Guards Army during the Battle of Kursk.

*Figure 63.* Soviet troops of the Voronezh Front counterattacking behind T-34 tanks at Prokhorovka during the Battle of Kursk

## Aftermath

In the middle of the battle, news arrived that the Allies had invaded Sicily. Even though Von Manstein believed they could still win, Hitler called off the operation and later moved much of his forces away from the Eastern Front.

Much like the Japanese defeat at Midway, after Kursk the Germans lost the ability to initiate major strategic offensive operations. From that point onwards, the German army was mostly on the defensive on the Eastern front. Even though the Russians losses in armor and aircraft were more than triple, the Germans couldn't win the war of attrition. Numbers came to bear—the Red Army simply had more resources and could easily replace losses.

# Operation Husky (Allied invasion of Sicily)

**July 9 to August 17, 1943**

**Belligerents:** Western Allies (United Kingdom, British India, United States, Canada, Free France, Australia, Italian citizens) vs. Germany and Italy

**Objective:** Invade Sicily

**Outcome:** Allies Capture Sicily

Operation Husky was the codename for the Allied invasion of Sicily during World War II. It was a large-scale amphibious operation that took place from July 9 to August 17, 1943. The objective of Operation Husky was to seize control of the island of Sicily from Axis forces, primarily Italian and German troops.

The invasion of Sicily was a critical step in the Allied strategy to liberate Italy and weaken Axis control over the Mediterranean region. By capturing Sicily, the Allies aimed to secure a base for launching further operations on the Italian mainland.

## Background

Even as the battle for North Africa was wrapping up, the Allies were already planning their next steps in the war.

The Americans wanted to attack France as soon as possible. British Prime Minister Churchill on the other hand, opposed a French landing at that point. Instead, he proposed an attack of Italy, which he described as the soft underbelly of Europe, and what he believed Germany's junior partner in the war. This is similar to his thinking in the First World War, when he advocated an attack on Turkey, the "weakest" in the Grand Alliance. The result was the Gallipoli or the Dardanelles campaign, which ultimately led to a Turkish victory.

Grudgingly, the Americans agreed to Churchill's suggestion to attack Sicily. If captured, it guaranteed almost total control of traffic in the Mediterranean while its proximity and airfields threatened the Italian mainland. This will also have the additional advantage of diverting Axis forces from the Eastern Front. In return, Churchill pledged more troops in Burma and the Pacific.

The Allies' primary target in the invasion of Sicily was the port of Messina. To do this, both US and British troops would land in Italy, though in separate beaches with different commanders.

**Figure 64.** A British soldier reads up on Sicily, the target for the next Allied invasion, July 1943.

## Operation

Under the command of British General Montgomery, four divisions consisting of British and Canadian soldiers were slated to carry out a landing operation at Syracuse, while on his left, American General Patton would lead three divisions in landing around Gela. In addition to these forces,

Free French units were also included in the two armies. As Montgomery spearheaded the advance towards Messina, Patton protected the flanks, with both generals reporting to British General Harold Alexander, forming a coordinated Allied effort in the Mediterranean theater.

This force was complemented by airborne troops who were assigned to capture bridges and other important installations.

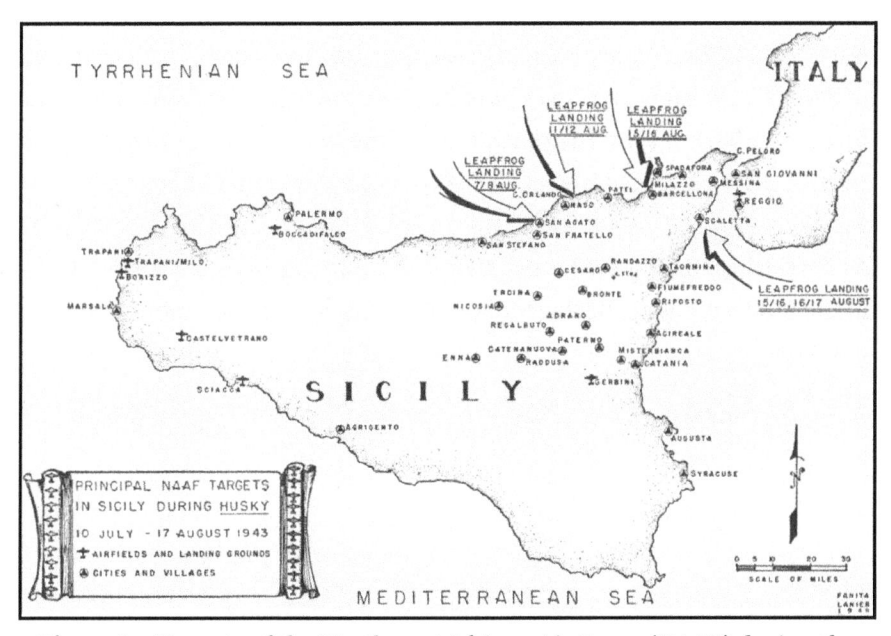

*Figure 65.* Targets of the Northwest African Air Force (NAAF) during the invasion of Sicily. Amphibious troops were to land at the island's southern part.

Thanks to Allied deception campaigns, the opposition at the beginning of the landings was lighter than expected. One of the most effective was Operation Mincemeat which convinced the Axis that Sicily was just a feint and the main attack was on Greece and the Balkans. Thus the Germans sent reinforcements to the latter.

With the exception of the Axis counterattack at Gela, the Allies faced minimal resistance until the British forces reached Catania. As Montgomery's advance became sluggish, he opted to use roads within the American sector, causing frustration for Patton. Seizing the opportunity, Patton initiated his own offensive, targeting the Axis right flank and successfully capturing Palermo, along with more than 50,000 Italian prisoners.

But German Field Marshal Albert Kesselring, known to the Allies as a master of defensive warfare took over. As reinforcements arrived from France, his forces fell back on the formidable Etna line with its terrain that heavily favored defenders. He also began the retreat to the Italian mainland.

As Kesselring completed the evacuation of 120,000 troops, Patton arrived at Messina several hours before Montgomery, completing the capture of Sicily.

OPERATION HUSKY (ALLIED INVASION OF SICILY)

*Figure 66.* A Universal carrier is towed ashore, as troops unload ammunition from a landing craft in the background, 10 July 1943.

## Aftermath

In the middle of the Sicily campaign, the Grand Council of Fascism voted to oust Italian dictator Benito Mussolini from his post. Despite assurances from Mussolini's successor, Hitler believed the Italians were defecting to the Allies. He began preparations to take over the country even as he canceled the operation at Kursk.

On the Allied side, they could sense victory now that Sicily was secured and Mussolini was no longer in power. They also heard whispers of Italians seeking peace. They were confident that Italy would soon fall. But it would be almost two years before the Allies completed the Italian campaign.

Patton's infamous slapping of soldiers suffering from PTSD also marked this campaign. High Command later broke his seventh army up and they transferred most of the units under his command to American general Mark Clark.

Some historians believed that had Patton kept command instead of Clark, the Italian campaign would've been shorter.

*Figure 67.* A wounded American soldier receiving blood plasma, Sicily, 9 August 1943. The soldier, Private Roy Humphrey from Ohio, died two days later in an Evacuation Hospital.

# Operation Eiche (The Gran Sasso Raid or the Rescue of Benito Mussolini)

*September 12, 1943*

**Belligerents:** Germany vs. Italy

**Objective**: Rescue Mussolini so he can be head of a new puppet Italian government

**Outcome:** Successful rescue of Mussolini.

## Background

In July 1943, after the Allied invasion of Sicily and the bombing of Rome, the Grand Council of Fascism voted a motion of no confidence against Prime Minister Benito Mussolini. He was arrested and replaced with Marshal Pietro Badoglio.

Although the Italians continued to fight alongside the Axis, they already began secret negotiations with the Allies to surrender, resulting in the Armistice of Cassibile. They also expected the Germans to attempt a takeover of the country and possibly reinstate Mussolini as head of an alternative government.

To prevent Mussolini falling into German hands, the Italians kept him at the Hotel Campo Imperatore. This was in a remote mountain plateau 2,112 meters above sea level and in the Gran Sasso d'Italia mountain range. Two hundred well-equipped Carabinieri guards watched him. The Italians

## OPERATION EICHE (THE GRAN SASSO RAID OR THE RESCUE OF BENITO...

believed the hotel was impregnable from a land attack.

**Figure 68.** Italian military and geo-political situation in September 1943. The northern half was governed by the Italian Socialist Republic, a Nazi-puppet government, while the second half was controlled by the Kingdom of Italy and the Allies.

## Operation

The operation was planned and executed by Fallschirmjäger Major Otto-Harald Mors and were joined by 16 SS troopers including Otto Skorzeny. The soldiers arrived by gliders towed by Henschel Hs 126 planes.

*Figure 69.* A German paratrooper (Fallschirmjäger) in front of a glider, at Gran Sasso.

Mors' group led the assault on the railway leading to the resort and cut off all communication lines. This action resulted in the deaths of two Italians—the only fatalities in the raid.

Skorzeny and the Fallschirmjäger troopers overwhelmed Mussolini's guards. They also had Italian General Fernando Soleti as a hostage. Soleti ordered the guards not to shoot.

The Germans escaped with both Mussolini and Soleti.

***Figure 70.*** Mussolini leaving the hotel at Gran Sasso with his German rescuers.

## Aftermath

Following the rescue, Mussolini was flown to Germany and was eventually installed as the figurehead leader of the Italian Social Republic, a German puppet state and collaborationist regime established in northern Italy.

Although the operation was planned, led, and executed by the Fallschirmjäger, German propaganda focused on Otto Skorzeny and the SS. The perception that Skorzeny led and executed the raid persists to this day.

The success of Operation Eiche did not significantly alter the course of the war, but it showcased the audacity and efficiency of German Special Forces. The operation remains one of the most notable and successful commando raids of World War 2.

# Operation Fortitude (Allied Deception Campaign for Normandy Landings)

*December 1943 to June 1944*

**Belligerents:** British and American Intelligence vs. Germany

**Objective:** Make the Germans believe that the main landings were at Pas de Calais or Norway. Keep German units stuck in the area and away from Normandy.

**Outcome:** Germany believed the Normandy landings were just a feint. They kept strong reserve units at the Pas de Calais area until July 1944.

Given England's proximity to France, the Germans knew it was just a matter of time when the Allies attempted an invasion. Traditionally, invaders from England usually landed at or near the Pas de Calais, the nearest point to England. The Germans thought this would not be an exception.

To reinforce this, the Allies launched Operation Bodyguard, which got its name from what Churchill said to Stalin — "the truth must have a bodyguard of lies." Bodyguard was the overall deception campaign for Overlord. One of its most major components was Operation Fortitude, convinced the Germans that the Allies were landing in either Norway or the Pas de Calais.

The Germans believed the ruse and kept forces in the north, away from the Normandy landing beaches. Even in July, the Germans thought the Normandy landings were just a diversion.

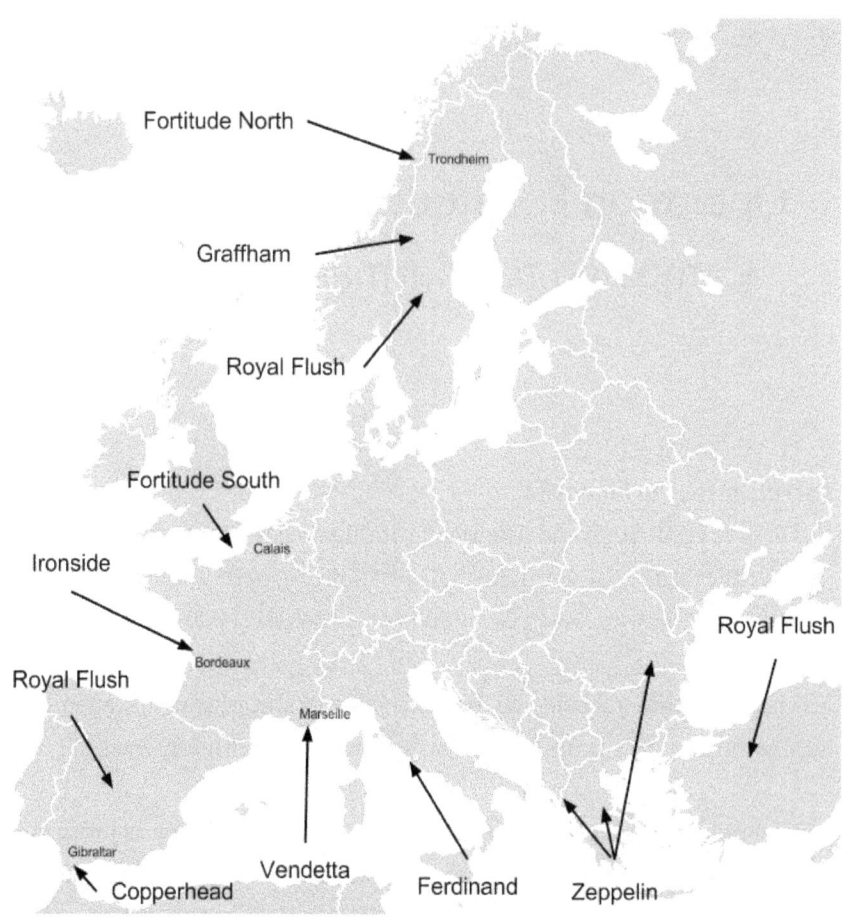

**Figure 71.** A map of the subordinate plans of Operation Bodyguard, the 1944 deception in support of the Allied invasion of Normandy (D-Day). Fortitude focused on Pas de Calais in France and Trondheim in Norway.

## Background

During the lead-up to the Normandy landings, the Allies devised a plan to mislead the Germans about when and where they were going to land. They had to believe that the landings at Normandy were just a feint and that the real one would come later, likely the Pas de Calais or even as far as Norway. This extra few days of confusion would mean the Germans' strongest forces and reserves are kept away from the beaches of Normandy.

## Operation

By 1944, Hitler was micromanaging everything about the war, rejecting the opinions of his most seasoned commanders. While he strongly believed that the landings would be at the Pas de Calais, he also knew the Allies could also adopt a more indirect route and land their forces as far as Norway. His Atlantic Wall, although still incomplete, was but a partial solution and the paranoia remained. Thus, if the Allies were to play mind games with someone, it only had to be Hitler. And Operation Fortitude invaded Hitler's mind.

Operation Fortitude focused on creating invasion threats all across the Atlantic Wall and beyond. It had two parts: North and South. South was focused on crossings on the English Channel. North was staged out of Scotland and appeared as a threat to as far as Norway.

### *Fortitude North*

For Fortitude North, the Allies aimed to mislead the Germans into expecting an invasion of Norway. They created a fictitious British Fourth Army based in Scotland. This was clever as there was once a real British Fourth Army, which was part of the British Expeditionary Force in World War 1. To add to the realism, British media broadcast fake sporting events and announcements related to the fourth Army.

**Figure 72.** Dummy landing craft used as decoys in south-eastern harbors in the period before D-Day.

To preserve the narrative, British commandos also attacked targets in Norway, destroying industrial and military targets as if to prepare for an invasion. The Allies also put additional political pressure on Sweden, implying that an attack on Norway was forthcoming.

This worked as Fortitude North tied down 13 army divisions in Norway.

### *Fortitude South*

Fortitude South was even more elaborate than Fortitude North. And like in the North, this operation mixed fact with fiction. The main fictional army for the invasion was the First United States Army Group or FUSAG. Like the British Fourth Army in the North, FUSAG was an actual unit, though mainly for administrative purposes. Thus the Germans were already familiar with the army in previous intercepts.

*Figure 73.* An inflatable Sherman tank decoy.

To add credence to the ruse, they assigned George Patton as head of FUSAG. He regularly appeared in the area for photographs, which were published in the papers. But the main part of the narrative was that FUSAG would land at the Pas de Calais, and everything else was a diversion.

Fortitude South had six sub-plans:

1. Leaks from Double Agents—Double agents will leak parts of the plans and reinforce the narrative about the Pas de Calais landings. This was done mainly with three agents code-named Garbo, Brutus, and Tricycle. Garbo was the most prominent and most critical among the three. He

actually sent a message just before dawn of June 6th about the Normandy landings. In an incredible stroke of luck, the radio operator did not process it until several hours later.
2. Simulated Wireless Traffic—The Allies will simulate increased traffic in the area. Sometimes, this involved trucks running along the beach, stopping at assigned points and sending assigned messages. Since the Luftwaffe was hardly present in the area, the Germans relied on captured and decrypted radio traffic.
3. Fake War Materiel and Infrastructure—The fake tanks, trucks, and materiel were not as extensive as Fortitude North, but fake buildings were also constructed. The Allies also built fake road signs, which will appear in photographs usually for the papers.
4. Attacks – Like in Fortitude North, this involved military activities such as bombing of the beaches at the Pas de Calais and the railway network. This intensified as D-Day approached. The general rule was bombing Pas de Calais with twice the number of bombs as Normandy.
5. Increased Movement—This meant increased activity in the area to suggest massive troop movement for the invasion. This was also true for support units.
6. Night Lighting—The night-lights from these activities could be seen from Pas de Calais, again giving the impression of extensive troop movements.

*Figure 74.* A dummy aircraft

## Aftermath

After the landings, the Allies kept the ruse alive, maintaining the narrative that FUSAG was still the main army. To explain the delay in the assault, they claimed the beaches were struggling, forcing Eisenhower to detach units from FUSAG and send them to Normandy. FUSAG would continue building strength and attack in July.

Operation Fortitude succeeded because it was a closed-loop operation, meaning the British controlled information reaching the Germans and they could also get feedback on how much the Germans believed.

German agents in Britain had been turned into double agents. Furthermore, the Japanese ambassador to Germany at the time revealed his personal conversations with the Hitler who believed the attack would definitely be at the Pas de Calais.

After the war, Garbo, the most successful double agent for the British, feared Nazi sympathizers might hunt him and his family. He faked his death and lived in Venezuela. Brutus stayed in the United Kingdom and published an account of his work during the war. Tricycle died in 1981 in France. He became the inspiration for a fictional British spy—James Bond.

# Operation Jericho (Amiens Prison Raid)

*February 18, 1944*

**Belligerents:** British, Australian, and New Zealand airmen working with the French resistance vs. Germany.

**Objective:** Liberate French resistance members, especially those who may knew about the invasion of France

**Outcome:** Dozens of French resistance members rescued, including those due for execution in days.

Operation Jericho, also known as the Amiens Prison Raid, was a daring and highly specialized mission conducted by the Royal Air Force (RAF) during World War II. It took place on February 18, 1944, and involved a precision bombing raid on the Amiens Prison in German-occupied France.

The aim of Operation Jericho was to breach the walls of the Amiens Prison and facilitate the escape of French Resistance fighters and other Allied prisoners held there. The raiders planned to disrupt German operations and morale, as well as providing support to the Resistance.

## Background

In 1943, the Gestapo and Abwehr had exposed spy networks active in France. This came at a critical time when the Allies were trying to get as much information about the Atlantic wall and the German units supporting it.

In February 1944, the Germans arrested Raymond Vivant, one of the last remaining free officers of the OCM. OCM or Organisation civile et militaire was a major resistance network in France. The Allies feared that if the Germans realized who he was, they might extract critical information from him.

The Allies had to break him out, along with other members of the French resistance.

## Operation

The first option was an armed raid by elite commando units, but this was abandoned as the Germans recently installed a permanent machine gun post and added eighty soldiers to guard the prison.

The next alternative was precision bombing aimed at the prison's walls and key military targets.

Leading the air assault was Group Captain Percy Charles Pickard, who was famous in England at the time for starring in the film Target for To-night. He led the group composed of Australian, New Zealanders, and British squadrons. Each mosquito carried four 500-lb bombs.

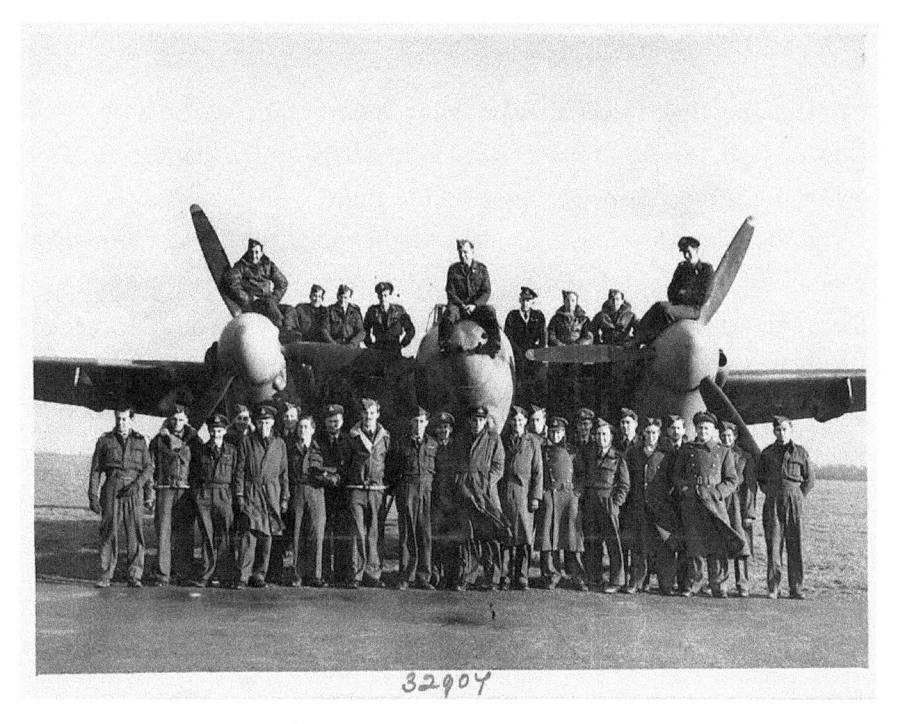

**Figure 75.** Mosquito and crew of the 487 (NZ) Squadron

The plan was to hit the adjoining guard quarters on both sides of the main prison. The British hoped the blasts would kill enough of the guards and the shock from the explosion would open the cell doors. Another group was also set to blast the prison walls surrounding the courtyard, giving the prisoners an exit. Outside, members of the French resistance are waiting with clothes, weapons, and fake IDs.

A coin toss decided the order of battle. The New Zealanders would make the first pass followed by the Australians. The British were on reserve just in case the previous planes failed to hit their targets. There was also support and air cover provided by fourteen Hawker Typhoons.

When the planes left the bases in England, they flew as close to the sea as possible. This continued when they reached France, as they flew near or at treetop levels. Sometimes, the planes even kicked out snow, as they were so near the ground.

Upon nearing their target, they initially aimed for the town of Albert before banking right towards Amiens. A straight road to Amiens connected Albert, giving the airmen the perfect bearing and guide.

The Australians and New Zealanders hit their targets. Soon, the airmen saw people rushing out of the prison. According to an RAF pilot, "You could tell them from the Germans because every time a bomb went off, the Germans would dive to the ground, but the prisoners kept on running like hell."

Towards the end of the mission, Pickard sent the signal "Red Daddy," the code that they did not need the British bombs and it's time to go. Unfortunately, a German fighter attacked him and destroyed his plane's tail. Pickard crashed and died.

*Figure 76.* Operation Jericho. A picture of the Amiens Prison taken shortly after the raid. Note the damaged buildings and the breached perimeter wall at the right. The ground is white due to the presence of snow.

## Aftermath

Based on official records, 102 prisoners died, 255 men escaped but 182 were recaptured The Allies believe the number of escapees to be higher. One reason is that two of the prisoners set some of the prison's records ablaze before escaping.

The escaped French resistance fighters later exposed 60 Gestapo agents and informers, thus inflicting serious damage on German counter-intelligence efforts.

Incredibly, there were no public accounts on what happened to Raymond Vivant.

# Operation Argument (Big Week or the Planned Destruction of the Luftwaffe)

*February 20 to 25, 1944*

**Belligerents:** United States and United Kingdom vs. Germany

**Objectives:** Cripple Germany's aircraft production capability. Destroy Luftwaffe fighters sent to defend these facilities.

**Outcome:** About one-third of Luftwaffe's existing fighters in the theater destroyed, along with about one-fifth of its pilots. Over 2,000 Dutch and German civilians were killed. Damage to airplane manufacturing facilities less than what Allies expected. Manufacturing operations transferred from the weak Air Ministry to Albert Speer's Armaments Ministry.

Upon seeing the new American B-17 bombers, a reporter from the Seattle times called it the flying fortress. And he had reason to. The American bombers were equipped with 10 or more .50-caliber machine guns and they believed that as long as they flew in tight formation, the Germans couldn't penetrate the cordon. Fighter escorts were just an additional luxury.

But by mid-1943, the Germans had shattered the concept of the impregnable Flying Fortress. Flak and aggressive fighters with heavier armaments wreaked havoc on the bombers. Worse, lack of range forced Allied fighter escorts to go back before the bombers reached their targets deep in Germany.

However, by early 1944, the Allied found a solution, mainly with the P-51 Mustang and its greater range.

## Background

One of the main prerequisites of the coming Operation Overlord was achieving air superiority. A nightmare scenario was a squadron of Luftwaffe fighters strafing the beaches full of troops and equipment.

The Allies decided they had to eliminate the Luftwaffe fighters as an effective fighting force. To do this, they adopted a "bait and kill" strategy. Bombers would attack the aircraft manufacturing facilities and act as bait to draw the German fighters. Once these appear, the Allied fighters would engage and massacre them. This was a new tactic as it was only recently that fighters with long ranges such as the P-51 Mustangs with drop tanks could join the bombers in their bombing runs.

Before the arrival of long-range fighters, the Allies avoided the Luftwaffe. Now, they were eager to face them. This new tactic later startled the German fighters as they saw Mustangs and even P-47 Thunderbolts deep into Germany.

Believing that the bombers were not as vulnerable as before, the Allies launched its biggest air operation yet—Operation Argument, better known as Big Week.

## Operation

The operation began with an air assault on several German targets: Leipzig, Bernberg, Rostock, Brunswick, Wilhelmtor, Neupetritor, and Oschersleben. The British and Americans alternated with the former bombing at night and the latter during the day.

The fighter escort's ability to join the bombers to their targets in Germany immediately paid dividends for the US Air Force. In one assault just outside of Hanover, a squadron of BF-110s was skimming the cloud cover and ready to pounce on the bombers. Unknown to them, P47 Thunderbolts lurked above.

When the Thunderbolts dove into the BF-110 formation, they shot 14 of 15 of the German fighters down with no losses.

This pattern would continue and by the end of the raid, Allied fighters had a more than 10:1 kill to death ratio. Towards the end of the raid, the Allies were using a tactic ordered by General Doolittle, wherein fighters detached themselves from the bombers and zoomed ahead, hunting for German fighters. This countered Germany's use of the Sturmböcke, a heavily armed Fw 190 designed to hunt bombers.

The weather in the next few days played a major factor in the operation, resulting in several missions being aborted or canceled. One of these aborted missions happened on February 22. The mission was aborted and a group of B-24 bombers looked for targets of opportunity on the way back. Unfortunately, some of the pilots thought they were still in Germany and aimed for a railway station, which after the attack was later correctly identified as the Nijmegen railway station. The bombers also bombed a residential area and destroyed several houses resulting in almost 1,000 Dutch civilians killed.

**Figure 77.** Damage to Nijmegen after the unintentional February 22 bombing of Nijmegen

More bad weather and the accidental bombing of civilians ultimately forced the Allies to pause and then call off the operation.

## Aftermath

The Germans lost about a third of their fighters and a fifth of their pilots in the theater. Losing the pilots was a serious setback for the Germans who were suffering similar losses in the Eastern front. Like the Japanese before them, they could not easily replace the experienced pilots.

The Allies on the other hand not only replaced their losses, but also increased their strength. They had twice the number of P-51 Mustangs by the end of the raid compared to when they began.

Another significant effect of the raid was the transfer of production from Hermann Göring's Air Ministry to Albert Speer's more effective Armaments Ministry. They split many of the factories into separate groups. This initially worked, but the Allies' non-stop attacks on the rail networks eventually ensured that the factories couldn't efficiently ship parts to each other.

# Operation U-Go (Japan's India Campaign)

*March to June 1944*

**Belligerents:** Japan and Azad Hind vs. the British Empire, mainly Indian troops

**Objective:** Capture the towns of Imphal and Kohima, and then the Brahmaputra Valley in India.

**Outcome:** British and Indian troops stop the Japanese.

Operation U-Go was among the last major offensives of Japan where it attempted to capture Northeast India, particularly the regions of Manipur and Assam. This resulted in two of the most savage and heroic episodes of the war—the battles of Imphal and Kohima.

## Background

In May 1942, the Japanese Army forced the Allies out of Burma. Like in Singapore they were heavily outnumbered but easily defeated the British and their allies. Surprisingly, the Japanese forces chose not to press further into India, opting to consolidate their gains in the theater instead. They believed the challenging terrain and potential supply difficulties in India were insurmountable, especially during the rainy season, which further hindered any offensive moves. As the Japanese forces maintained a defensive stance, the Allies strategically constructed several airbases in the Assam region to support and supply the Chinese forces.

## OPERATION U-GO (JAPAN'S INDIA CAMPAIGN)

However, the dynamics shifted with the establishment of the Burma Area Army, led by Lieutenant General Masakazu Kawabe. One of his commanders, Lieutenant-General Renya Mutaguchi, was an advocate of a more aggressive approach. Mutaguchi devised a daring plan to advance to the Brahmaputra Valley, effectively cutting off the Allies' supply lines to Burma. This ambitious move also entailed neutralizing the Allied airfields, which served as the primary source of supplies to sustain China's participation in the fight against the Japanese.

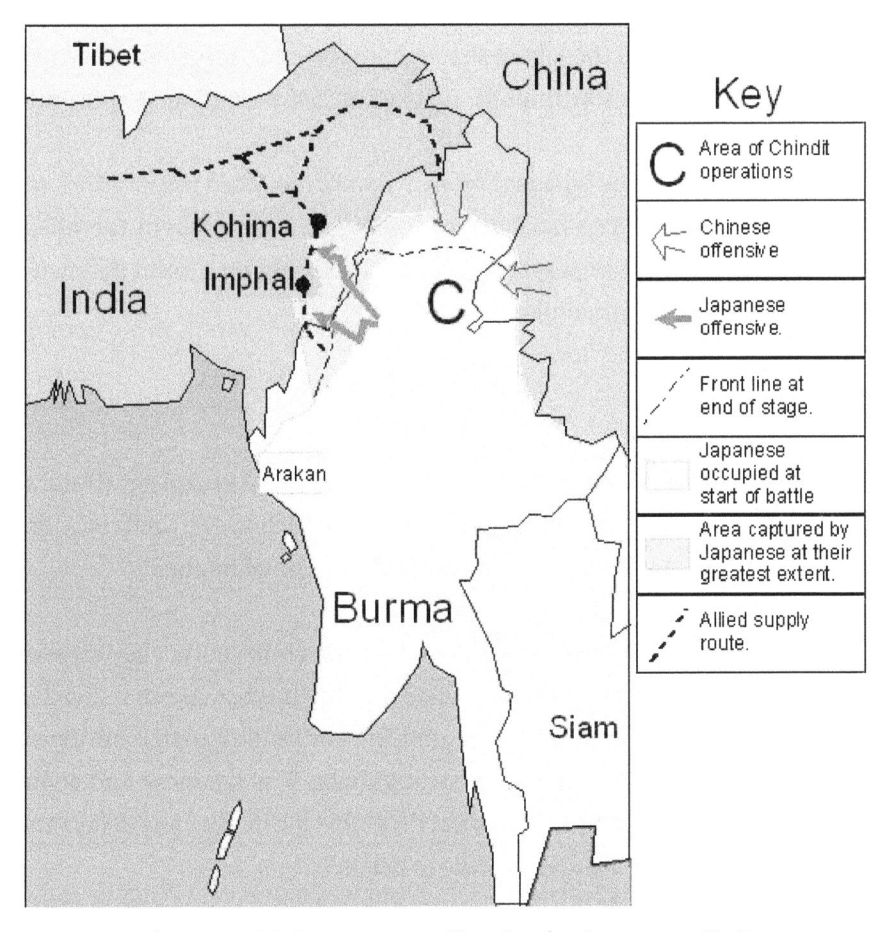

*Figure 78.* Main Japanese offensive for Operation U-Go.

The Azad Hind, the Japanese-sponsored provisional government in India supported them. Azad Hind was led by Subhas Bose, an Indian nationalist known for defying British authority in India and now a supporter of the Japanese Army.

Bose believed the Indians were tired of British rule. He claimed that Indians serving in the British Army would refuse to fight and change sides when they come across Azad Hind's Indian National Army (INA). After all, most of the members of the INA Indians were either volunteers or POWs from the Battle of Singapore. There was also historical precedence for this as in 1942, a huge chunk of the Burmese population supported the Japanese in ousting the British.

Bose also convinced the Japanese to incorporate two brigades of the INA to be at the front lines at Imphal, instead of just providing support and reconnaissance.

Adding urgency to the Japanese offensive were the Allied preparations for an attack on Burma. The Japanese believed that if they caught the Allied armies, dispersed while preparing to attack and not on a solid defensive formation, they could annihilate them.

## Operation

To mask their true targets, the Japanese planned a diversionary attack at Arakan about 400 miles away. This eventually failed, however, and the Allies were later able to fly a division to help in the defense of Imphal.

On March 6, General Mutaguchi led two divisions into India. They crossed the Chindwin River and advanced quickly towards Imphal. Another division proceeded directly to Kohima, bringing in over 80,000 battle-hardened infantry advancing toward British strongholds. The Japanese had about a month's worth of supplies. This tight timetable meant that any delays and the Japanese army would starve while in battle.

The Japanese launched a successful attack on the scattered Allied army as they were gearing up for their own offensive. In response, the Allied forces retreated and regrouped, establishing a defensive perimeter in Imphal. Meanwhile, in the northern front, the Japanese also targeted Kohima, unaware of the presence of a paratrooper unit training in the nearby jungle. The paratroopers held their ground for an impressive six days, providing the Allies with vital time to reinforce Kohima and fortify the defenses at Imphal.

*Figure 79.* Soldiers of the Imperial Japanese Army advance during Operation U-Go

By April 5, the Japanese had severed the road between Imphal and Kohima, leading the Allies to provide garrison reinforcement through airdrops which often missed their targets and were not enough. The Japanese managed to capture supply depots along the way, albeit with limited food supplies. Both sides endured a war of attrition, with the Kohima garrison enduring constant Japanese artillery attacks, but ultimately, fresh troops relieved the defenders after over two weeks, while the dwindling Japanese forces had no reinforcements to rely upon.

At Imphal, the situation was precarious as in early April, the Allies suffered attacks and were on the verge of collapse. On April 13, the Allies counterattacked at Nungshigum ridge, which overlooked the Imphal airstrip. The allies bombarded the area with artillery and air strikes before sending in infantry backed up by M3 Lee tanks.

The Allies also counter-attacked at Kohima and drove the Japanese from their positions, though the latter continued to hold on to the critical Imphal-Kohima road. However, by May 22, the road was open once more. And on June 22, the Allied armies ended the Siege of Imphal.

By early July, the Japanese had retreated. Estimates of Japanese who died ranged from 13,000 to 55,000 with about half of that from disease and starvation.

Ten months later, the Allies liberated Rangoon, the capital of Burma with Operation Dracula.

## Aftermath

After the war, General Mutaguchi relieved most of the senior officers under his command, before being relieved himself in August. Mutaguchi's ire was directed at Lieutenant General Kotoku Sato, head of the Japanese army at Kohima who withdrew without orders. Sato's men were dying of starvation and were running out of ammunition. High Command expected Sato to commit seppuku, but he declined and requested court martial to clear his name and voice his criticisms against Mutaguchi. He was later declared unfit to stand trial. Two of Sato's criticisms against Mutaguchi were the latter's inability or refusal to supply the Army. He was also critical of the order to transfer troops fighting in Kohima to Imphal even as they struggled.

After the war, Sato struggled with accusations of cowardice and incompetence but defended himself saying he did what he could to save his starving and unsupplied men.

The failure of Operation U-Go signaled the end of major Japanese offensives in the Burmese theater. Once the Allies had rested and refitted, the Allies attacked, culminating in Operation Dracula, the mission to liberate Rangoon.

Operation U-Go was one of those campaigns that could've significantly altered the course of the war. By winning, the Allies ensured the continuous re-supply of the Chinese Nationalists and stopped further incursions to India. Had the Japanese won, they could've captured the airbases and China would have had a serious supply problem. The road to India would've been clear. There was also the chance, as Bose claimed, that the Indians would rise against their British colonizers.

# Operation Ichi-Go (Japanese offensive in China)

***April 19 to December 31, 1944***

*Belligerents:* Japan vs. China and the United States (air support only)

*Objectives:* Create a land-route for a re-invasion of French Indochina, capture airbases, capture key Chinese cities and consolidate captured territories, thus weakening Chinese resistance.

*Outcome:* Japanese Pyrrhic victory. Weakening of Chiang's National Revolutionary Army.

OPERATION ICHI-GO (JAPANESE OFFENSIVE IN CHINA)

*Figure 80.* Evacuation of Liuchow, November 1944. It was captured by the Japanese army on 7 November 7,1944 during the Battle of Guilin–Liuzhou

## Background

Operation Ichi-Go was a major military operation conducted by the Imperial Japanese Army in 1944 during World War II. It was a series of coordinated offensives launched in China with the objective of capturing strategic territories, securing resources, and ultimately dealing a severe blow to Chinese resistance.

Generalissimo Chiang Kai Shek, leader of the Chinese Nationalist Army, did not anticipate this attack, underestimating the Japanese' capacity for a major offensive as he believed they had diverted their troops to support Operation U-Go in India and were not prepared for another significant assault.

*Figure 81.* A Type 97 ShinHoTo Chi-Ha tank of the 3rd Tank Division of the Imperial Japanese Army operating at night during the Operation Ichi-gō in northern China, December 1944

## Operation

The operation was composed of three major battles: the battles of Central Henan, Changheng, and Guilin-Liuzhou.

### Battle of Central Henan

Chinese General Tang Enbo and his 390,000 soldiers dug in to reinforce the ancient city of Luoyang. The Japanese adopted an indirect approach, using armor as the 3rd Tank Division flanked the Chinese. First, they went around the Yellow River in the Zhengzhou area then defeated the Chinese near Xuchang. Finally, they swung around clockwise and besieged Luoyang. By May 25, the city was in Japanese hands and virtually controlled the province of Henan.

### *Battle of Changsha*

This battle started almost immediately after the Japanese victory at Henan. On May 27, the Japanese quickly overwhelmed the defending Chinese at Changsa. However, the Japanese experienced unexpected heavy resistance at Hengyang. Led by General Fang Xianjue, a force of 17,000 Chinese defenders held out against the over 100,000 Japanese attackers for 47 days. This delay also led to the collapse of the ruling coalition in Japan as it forced Prime Minister Hideki Tojo to resign.

### *Battle of Guilin-Liuzhou*

In this battle, the Japanese primary goal was to consolidate the earlier gains of Operation Ichi-go. A secondary objective was destroying US air bases.

Japan's 11th and 23rd armies launched attacks against the cities of Guilin and Liuzhou. Ten days later, despite fierce resistance, the two cities fell marking the end of Operation Ichi-go. However, despite their success in capturing the urban centers, the Japanese failed to gain control over the surrounding rural areas, as heightened Chinese activity thwarted any further territorial expansion and movement.

*Figure 82.* Japanese troops performing advancing during an attack on the Yüeh-Han Railroad.

### Henan Peasants Attack Kuomintang Forces

Probably the most unexpected incident during the campaign was when peasants from Western Henan attacked the Kuomintang Forces. They not only stole weapons and equipment, and the army's food, they also killed soldiers, especially officers.

One explanation is this was revenge for the Yellow River flood and the Chinese famine of 1942-43. During this time, the Kuomintang forcibly took food from the civilians to feed the army, leaving the people to starve to death. According to estimates, about 700,000 people died during the famine.

## Aftermath

Ichi-Go was a Japanese victory, although a pyrrhic one as they lost over 100,000 men. While they achieved their initial objective of forcing the American bombers from their bases, Allied victories in Marianas meant the US could still bomb the same Japanese targets, but from other locations. Their capture of the cities and not much of the surrounding rural areas also limited the effect of their victory. They could not move around without fear of an ambush by the Chinese.

There was also a major shift in the relationship between the US and Chiang. Commander of US forces General Stillwell, with support from Washington, demanded that he be placed in unrestricted command of all Chiang's forces. All this even as he remained Chief of Staff to Chiang. Chiang acquiesced to this demand, but only with the condition that a general other than Stillwell would assume the post.

Probably the biggest winners of this operation were the Communist Chinese guerillas. After General Stillwell's recall, the pro-Chiang Allied press censorship was no longer as strict. There were more stories that painted Chiang's Nationalist forces as incompetent and corrupt. As the Nationalists became unpopular and their forces became weaker, the Chinese Communists gained support, which continued after World War 2. Thus, the unintended effect of Operation Ichi-Go was helping in the eventual Communist victory in the Chinese Civil War which resumed after Japan's surrender.

# Operation Diadem (Battle of the Liri Valley or the Fourth Battle of Monte Cassino)

*May 11 to June 4, 1944*

**Belligerents:** Western Allies (Including Free France, Poland, and Canada) vs. Germany and the Italian Socialist Republic

**Objectives:** Break the Gustav line and open up the Liri Valley, thus opening the road to Rome.

**Outcome:** The Allies break the Axis lines.

## Background

Contrary to Churchill's portrayal of Italy as the "soft underbelly of Europe," the capture or liberation of Italy proved to be a formidable and prolonged undertaking, lasting nearly 22 months until May 1945. Operation Diadem, also known as the Fourth Battle of Monte Cassino, emerged as a significant offensive in the Italian Campaign, to break through the German Gustav Line and capture strategic locations like Monte Cassino and the Liri Valley.

Primarily under the command of General Sir Harold Alexander and his subordinate General Mark W. Clark, the multinational force of American, British, French, Canadian, and Polish troops pressed forward with the objective of opening a pathway to Rome and advancing up the Italian peninsula. As a secondary goal, the campaign sought to tie down German forces in Italy, limiting their deployment to France during Operation Overlord in June 1944.

## Operation

Operation Diadem began when the British 4th Infantry Division, the 8th Indian Brigade supported by the 1st Canadian Armored Brigade crossed the Garigliano and Rapido rivers. This assault broke German defenses at the Liri Valley.

Probably the specially trained French Corps led by General Alphonse Juin conducted the most impressive attack. Juin's troops, which included Moroccan Gourmiers showed their expertise in mountain warfare, overcoming terrains that the Germans thought were impregnable. American general Mark Clark later said the French Corps' performance provided the difference between victory and defeat.

*Figure 83.* A Moroccan Goumier sharpening his bayonet. Italy 1944. Gourmiers played a key role in breaking Germany's Gustav Line.

And while the French were knocking out parts of the Gustav line, the US II Corps attacked along the coast, and the Polish II Corps attacked Monte Cassino.

When the Gustav line collapsed, the Germans retreated to the Hitler line.

## Aftermath

Operation Diadem was a turning point in the Italian Campaign, as it effectively broke the German defensive lines and enabled the Allies to push northward. While it would almost be a year before the Germans and their allies were defeated in Italy, this operation led to the fall of Rome, the first Axis capital city to do so.

A major controversy in this operation was Mark Clark's refusal to follow Harold Alexander's direct order to cut the German's line of retreat. Instead, Clark ordered the US VI Corps to advance to Rome. Clark's refusal to follow the direct order had dire consequences. The German Tenth Army could've been destroyed or captured. Instead, the Allies had to fight them in the next few months, doubling their casualties.

According to many historians, General Mark W. Clark's decision to capture Rome was driven by his desire for his own army to achieve the feat instead of the British forces advancing from the Liri Valley. While Clark ultimately entered Rome as its liberator, this move allowed the German Tenth Army to escape.

Despite the high cost of his entry to Rome, Clark's moment of glory was fleeting. Just two days later, Operation Overlord would dominate the headlines.

# Operation Overlord (D-Day or the Allied invasion of Normandy)

*June 6 to August 30, 1944*

**Belligerents:** United States, United Kingdom, Canada, France, Poland, Australia, New Zealand, Netherlands, Belgium, Norway, Czechoslovakia, Luxembourg, Greece, Southern Rhodesia, South Africa vs. Germany, Italian Socialist Republic

**Objectives:** Establish beachhead in Normandy, Liberate most of France

**Outcome:** Successful landing in Normandy. Paris was liberated on August 19, 1944. Allies advancing all over Western Europe.

Operation Overlord was the codename for the Allied invasion of Normandy during World War II. It was a massive amphibious assault launched on June 6, 1944 or D-Day, with the objective of liberating German-occupied Western Europe and ultimately defeating Nazi Germany.

Under the overall command of General Dwight D. Eisenhower, Operation Overlord involved the coordinated efforts of American, British, Canadian, and other Allied forces.

The operation began with a massive aerial and naval bombardment of German coastal defenses to soften them up prior to the amphibious landings. The Allies also dropped thousands of paratroopers behind enemy lines to secure key objectives and disrupt German defenses.

On the morning of D-Day, Allied forces stormed the beaches of Normandy in five designated landing zones: Utah, Omaha, Gold, Juno, and Sword. The American forces landed at Utah and Omaha, while the British and Canadians landed in the other beaches. The landings faced heavy resistance from German troops, fortified positions, and obstacles, but the Allies established beachheads and pushed inland.

Despite initial challenges, the Allied forces gradually expanded their foothold in Normandy and successfully broke out from the beachheads. By the end of August, much of France was liberated. Belgium would follow in less than a week and the Allies were advancing all over Europe.

Operation Overlord marked a significant turning point in the war. With the landings in France, Germany was now fighting a war on three major fronts: the Eastern Front, the Western Front, and Italy.

## Background

Following the successful evacuation at Dunkirk, the somber Allies knew that eventually, they needed to embark on another cross-channel operation to liberate France. In early 1942, the US put forth two proposals: Operation Roundup, a 1943 invasion of France, and Operation Sledgehammer, aiming to capture a major French port during early autumn of 1942 if either Germany or the Soviet Union faced imminent collapse.

However, the British opposed a cross-channel invasion at that time, persuading the Americans to instead pursue Operation Torch. They argued the Allies lacked air superiority, sufficient forces, and proper equipment for such an ambitious attack. Additionally, the ongoing Battle of the Atlantic posed a threat to supply lines, making the alternative Operation Torch a more workable choice for the time being.

In the wake of successful landings in North Africa, followed by invasions of Sicily and mainland Italy, the British again attempted to suppress talks of a cross-channel invasion in 1943.

In the May 1943 Washington Conference code-named Trident, Churchill continued to vacillate about a cross-channel invasion. He argued for the postponement of the invasion for at least a year to give them ample time to bolster troop strength, manufacture vehicles, weapons, and other essential supplies required for the landings.

In the Tehran Conference of November 1943, however, things changed. Both US President Franklin Roosevelt and Soviet leader Joseph Stalin exerted pressure on British Prime Minister Winston Churchill to agree wholeheartedly to the invasion, which was set for May 1944. As part of the agreement, Stalin also pledged to launch a major offensive also around that time, which would eventually be Operation Bagration.

General Dwight D. Eisenhower was appointed as the commander of the Supreme Headquarters Allied Expeditionary Force (SHAEF), while a British General was assigned to lead the land forces in the impending invasion. These pivotal decisions set the stage for the momentous D-Day invasion and Bagration.

British Lieutenant General Frederick Morgan was appointed Chief of Staff, Supreme Allied Commander (COSSAC) and began planning the invasion. Four sites were considered for the landings: Brittany, the Cotentin Peninsula (also known as Cherbourg Peninsula), Normandy, and the Pas de Calais. He began plans for Overlord, which included the early details of both Operation Roundup and Sledgehammer and a combination of the two, Operation Roundhammer.

Among these four, the most tempting targets were Cherbourg and Brittany because of their harbors. This, however, meant they were more heavily defended, thus the Allies rejected them. Moreover, their geographic locations meant the Germans could stop the Allied advance over a narrow front. Pas de Calais was an obvious choice as it was nearest to the British Isles. However, it also meant it contained probably the strongest section of the Atlantic Wall. Ultimately, the planners selected Normandy because it was close enough that the Allies could have air superiority over the landing sites. They also expected it to be less defended than the other three. Aside from these, a successful landing at Normandy would enable them to threaten the ports of Brittany and Cherbourg.

The only drawback against Normandy was its lack of harbors. This was also the reason the Germans thought landings here were unlikely, as the Allies needed a port to bring in supplies for an invasion. If the Allies could not supply their forces, they could not advance beyond the initial beachhead and are vulnerable to counterattack. To solve this, the British designed the Mulberry Harbor, an artificial and temporary harbor that could last long enough until the Allies captured a deep-water port.

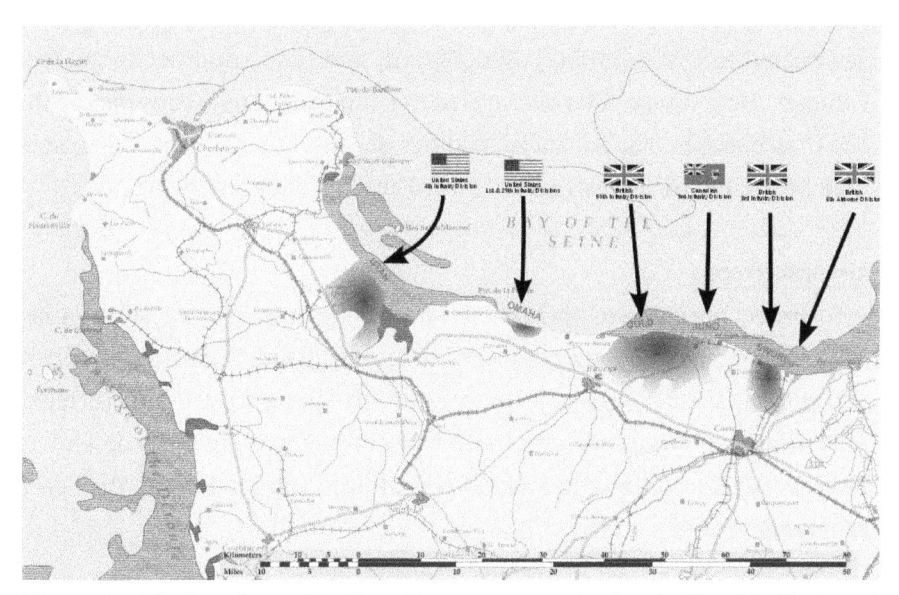

*Figure 84.* The beaches of D-Day. Paratroopers also landed beside Utah and Sword to protect the Allies' flanks.

## Operation

Operation Overlord was a complex military operation that involved a lot of moving parts. They culminated in the landings on June 6, 1944.

### *Operation Neptune*

Operation Neptune was the codename for the amphibious landings and airborne operations on June 6, 1944 in the Allied invasion of Normandy. It is probably the best known sub-operation of Operation Overlord. It was the start of Operation Overlord and is often referred to as D-Day.

This operation involved landing in five beaches along the Normandy coast designated as Utah, Omaha, Gold, Sword, and Juno. Another target was Pointe du Hoc, whose cliffs overlooked the English Channel between Omaha and Utah beaches. The advanced landings of American paratroopers west of Utah beach and the British east of Sword beach supported them.

### *Airborne Troops*

To protect the flanks of the invasion and to delay counter-attacks, the Allies deployed an airborne force composed of American and British paratroopers and glider infantry. Their objective was to seize key infrastructure (bridges, roads, canals, crossroads, etc.) and sow confusion among the defenders. They were to hold these key sections until infantry landing on the beach could relieve them.

Elements of the US 82nd and 101st Airborne Divisions were assigned objectives west of Utah Beach where they hoped to capture the four major causeways leading from the beach. In the eastern flank, the British 6th Airborne Division was assigned to capture intact (Caen Canal Bridge) Pegasus and (River Orne Bridge) Horsa bridges, destroy five other bridges, and destroy the Merville Gun Battery overlooking Sword Beach. The British paratroopers achieved all their objectives, though the Germans recaptured the gun battery after they left. Some paratroopers in the British airborne unit were members of the Free French who were assigned objectives in Brittany.

*Figure 85.* A paratrooper from the US 101st Airborne Division climbing aboard the lead transport aircraft C-47 Dakota at RAF Exeter Airfield, Devon, the UK on the night of 5/6th June 1944 for a drop behind Utah Beach on the Cotentin Peninsula of France.

The US paratroopers were scattered but rallied to reach most of their objectives. Soldiers from the 101st Division performed one of the most famous and studied assaults during D-Day—the assault on Brecourt Manor, where 23 paratroopers overcame 60 German defenders and destroyed four Howitzers firing at Utah Beach.

### Utah Beach

Utah Beach was located at the westernmost area of the Normandy beach landings. It is the landing section closest to the Cotentin Peninsula, which contains the important port of Cherbourg. The Cotentin area was originally an option as the main landing area on D-Day, but was ultimately rejected because it was a peninsula, and the Germans might bottle up the Allies in a small area. Thus, one of the latter objectives of the forces landing at Utah was to cut off Cherbourg from reinforcements, and then capture the port.

*Figure 86.* US soldiers landing on Utah Beach. Note the destroyed vehicles ahead.

The landing force of 21,000 men was composed primarily of elements of the US 4th Infantry Division and the 70th Tank Battalion. About 14,000 paratroopers from the US 82nd and 101st Airborne Divisions supported them.

The paratroopers were dispersed but were eventually able to control the key crossroads at and near Sainte-Mère-Église. They were also able to easily capture 2 of the 4 causeways or exit points from the beaches at Utah. This came at a high price though as they had casualties of over 2,000.

The landing troops attacked in four waves and captured the beachhead with minimal casualties. The bocage hindered their later attempts to break out, but the casualties were lower than expected at 197 killed.

### Omaha Beach

Omaha Beach was the second beach from the west that the Allies attacked on D-Day. It was also the largest, stretching over 6 miles (10 km) between Port-en-Bessin and the Vire River. The landing beaches were wide enough for two regiments to land side by side.

*Figure 87.* Elements of the US Army's First Division disembark from An LCVP (Landing Craft, Vehicle, Personnel) on the morning of June 6, 1944 (D-Day) at Omaha Beach.

Omaha was the most heavily defended beach on D-Day, as half of the troops manning it were battle-hardened. Worse, almost everything went wrong in the landings. Strong currents swept the landing crafts and were either dispersed or landed far from the target area. Armor supporting it had difficulty reaching the beach, with the armor arriving after the infantry instead of before as planned. The first batch of 29 DD tanks was all swamped while wading ashore. There were other losses in armor in the next batches and only 19 made it off the beach, all of them arriving late in the battle. The situation was so uncertain that at some point, General Omar Bradley considered evacuating Omaha.

Throughout the landing, German gunners poured deadly fire into the ranks of the invading Americans. The slaughter was such that a German officer concluded they had stopped the landings. But the men kept on coming and soon most of the Germans' MG-42s ran low on ammunition. Small groups of men began climbing the cliffs and assaulting the defenses. The destroyers McCook and Frankford who began firing from as close as 1,000 yards (910 m) helped them.

Amidst all the chaos, General Norman Cota was on the beach and rallied the pinned down survivors. He calmly told his troops, "Gentlemen, we are being killed on the beaches. Let us go inland and be killed." In another instance, trying to inspire the Rangers to leave cover and advance, Cota declared, "Rangers lead the way!" This eventually became the motto of the US Army Rangers. By noon, German fire had decreased significantly and the American infantry attacked the defensive strongpoints from the rear.

By nightfall, the Allies had landed 34,000 men at Omaha. It was a costly day with over 2,400 Allied casualties and the Germans suffering half of that.

### *Gold Beach*

Gold Beach was in the middle of the five landing areas, between Port-en Bessin and the Lieu-dit La Rivière. Capturing Gold Beach was the responsibility of the 50th British Infantry. The British's goal was to capture Arromanches, Bayeux, and Port-en-Bessin. They were also supposed to link up with the Americans in Omaha and the Canadians in Juno, creating a contiguous beachhead. They were to land into two sections: King and Jug.

Unlike at Omaha, the infantry, engineers, and supporting DD tanks landed at the same time at the beach's King Sector. But the Germans had fortified several houses and La Rivière, and the infantry supported by tanks had to clear them all morning.

At the Jig sector, because of errors and the tide coming in earlier than expected, the forces either missed their intended landing areas or arrived late.

By nightfall, 25,000 soldiers had landed. The Allies captured Arromanches in the afternoon, with Bayeux and Port-en-Bessin falling the following day. They were also able to link up with the Canadians who landed at Juno.

### *Juno*

Juno was the sector between Gold and Sword beaches. It was close to the size of Omaha at 6 miles (10 km) wide and spanned from Courseulles to Saint-Aubin-sur-Mer. The First Canadian Army was tasked with taking the sector. Their main objectives were to cut the Caen-Bayeux road, seize the Carpiquet Airfield and link between the two landings at Sword and Gold.

*Figure 88.* LCA (Landing Craft Assault) containing Winnipeg Rifles head for the Normandy Juno beach - June 6, 1944.

The German 716th Infantry Division defended the area with the 21st Panzer Division in reserve. Critically for the attackers, the Panzers couldn't be released without Hitler's explicit permission.

But the Canadians landed three hours after the optimum rising tide. Because of this, the beach obstacles were already submerged, and the mines were no longer visible. This resulted in about 30% of the landing craft destroyed or damaged.

One out of two soldiers landing in the first wave became casualties. But by mid-morning, the towns of Bernières and Saint-Aubin were occupied.

But once again, the DD tanks arrived late, leaving the task of eliminating enemy strongpoints to the infantry. In the assault on the Bernières-sur-Mer seawall, the costliest single battle on Juno Beach, elements of the Queen's Own Rifles and Quebec's Régiment de la Chaudière overcame the defenses without the aid of armor.

While the Canadian forces made significant advancements compared to other landing forces during the D-Day invasion, they faced criticism for their failure to capture Carpiquet Airfield. This setback was partially caused by delays experienced by the British forces at Sword beach. Additionally, moving forward would have left their flanks vulnerable, as reports of German 21st Panzer movement emerged, warranting caution. Amidst the uncertainty, reports of an imminent German counter-attack led Lieutenant-General Miles Dempsey to order forces at Sword, Juno, and Gold beaches to establish defensive positions at their intermediate objectives. Carpiquet Airfield was eventually captured a month later as part of Operation Windsor.

By the end of D-Day, 21,400 Canadians had landed with casualties of 340 killed and 574 wounded. They had also advanced farther than any other Allied unit.

**Sword**
Sword beach covered 5 miles (8 km) from Ouistreham to Saint-Aubin-sur-Mer, It was the easternmost landing site after a sixth beach, codenamed Band, was canceled. The Allies suffered the fewest casualties at Sword Beach, but delays and congestion on the beaches and a strong German counterattack prevented them from capturing the main objective of Caen.

By noon, the British had joined the paratroopers at Pegasus Bridge and Ranville. At the end of D-Day, the British were just over 3 miles (4.8 km) from Caen. Of the 28,845 men who landed, almost 700 became casualties.

*Figure 89.* Royal Marine Commandos attached to 3rd Division move inland after landing at Sword Beach. A Churchill bridgelayer can be seen in the background.

### *Pointe Du Hoc*

Pointe Du Hoc was a 100-foot (30 m) tall promontory west of Omaha Beach. It gave the Germans a commanding view of the beaches, and spotters could easily identify targets for the artillery further inland.

Though planned separately, the assault was a part of the operations at Omaha.

On D-Day, Army rangers scaled the cliffs and assaulted the German 155 mm guns threatening both Omaha and Utah.

A battleship and three destroyers provided suppressing fire to prevent the Germans from attacking the climbing rangers.

The original force was supposed to be reinforced by a larger group of 8 companies of Rangers. But the signals from the original force arrived too late, and this reinforcement was already diverted to Omaha Beach. According to some historians, this ultimately benefited the allies as the group prevented the Omaha landings from being a disaster. The Rangers led the assault beyond the beach and into German defenses.

*Figure 90.* U.S. Army Rangers with the ladders they used to storm the cliffs at Pointe du Hoc on D-Day.

The Rangers had fifteen casualties on the beach and another 15 when they took Pointe du Hoc. They also found out that the guns, which were their main objectives, were not there. However, a small patrol later found the guns and disabled them with thermite grenades.

By the time they were relieved, only 90 out of the 225 men were available to fight.

Years later, declassified files revealed that Ranger commander Colonel James Rudder knew before the landings that the Germans had moved the guns, replaced with wooden telephone poles resembling artillery.

## Operation Dragoon

Operation Dragoon, the invasion of Southern France, was originally planned to coincide with D-Day but lack of resources resulted in its postponement. In July, however, the Allies were having serious supply problems. A storm destroyed one of the Mulberry harbors, while the retreating Germans sabotaged the port at Cherbourg. As a result, the Allies revisited the plans with the aim of forcing the Germans to fight in Southern France, and then capture the port facilities at Marseilles and Toulon.

On August 15, the Allies launched Operation Dragoon. They liberated Toulon on August 26. Marseilles followed two days later. By the end of the operation in mid-September, over 17,000 Allied soldiers had been killed (7301 Americans and over 10,000 French). The Germans suffered 7,000 killed and over 130,000 captured.

## Deception

To hide their actual intentions, the Allies launched Operation Bodyguard. The Allies made sure that they kept the Germans guessing on the when and where the landings would take place. To do this, they had a network of agents reinforce Germany's belief that the landings would come at the Pas de Calais, just opposite of Dover.

The Allies created fictitious armies and radio traffic to deceive the Germans. They also bombed the Pas de Calais with twice the number of bombs compared to Normandy. They wanted Hitler to believe that the landings at Normandy were just a feint and the actual target was the Pas de Calais.

This ruse worked and even in July, Hitler refused to release the reserves stationed at the Pas de Calais.

### *Weather*

The initial weather forecasts indicated stormy conditions during the first week, which aligned with the German assessment, leading them to believe an attack was unlikely. This confidence in German forecast was so high that Erwin Rommel left France for Germany to attend his wife's birthday.

Despite Eisenhower initially setting June 5 as the invasion date, the storms persisted, posing risks for the larger ships. However, English weather forecasters provided a glimmer of hope, advising Eisenhower that the weather would briefly improve, allowing for an invasion on June 6th. Trusting his meteorologist, Eisenhower seized the opportunity during a window of relative calm, with relatively clear skies though the seas remained rough, and launched Operation Overlord.

### *Breakout*

Montgomery continued the pressure on the Eastern side of the beachhead, focusing his attention on Caen. He launched Operation Goodwood, a failed attack to take Caen. In this battle, the Allies lost over 400 tanks.

On the Western side of the beachhead, General Omar Bradley launched Operation Cobra, taking advantage of the Germans' focus on Montgomery and Operation Goodwood. The aerial bombardment involved one of the most notorious friendly fire episodes of the war. But the subsequent infantry and armor assault was successful. By August 4, Patton's newly activated Third had swept through Avranches and into Brittany.

## Aftermath

While it's now easy to look at D-Day as a success, it wasn't a sure thing in 1944. Allied planners had feared that at least half of the airborne would be casualties. Even Eisenhower had a separate statement just in case the operation failed. During the early hours at Omaha, General Bradley struggled with the option of pausing the assault and diverting forces intended there to another beach. By the end of the first day, the Allies had also failed to capture key objectives: Caen, Carentan, Bayeux, and Isigny-sur-Mer. Except for Juno and Gold, the five beaches remained isolated and all remained vulnerable.

Still the Allied had a beachhead in France. And it would only expand in the coming days. The Western front that Hitler had feared had arrived.

# Operation Bagration (Soviet Offensive on the Eastern Front)

**June 22 to August 19, 1944**

**Belligerents:** Soviet Union and Poland vs. Germany, Hungary, and Romania

**Objectives:** Liberate Belorussia, isolate the three German Army Groups from each other

**Outcome:** Belorussia liberated. Army Group Center Annihilated, Army Group North cut off for the rest of war.

Operation Bagration was a major Soviet military offensive during World War II, launched on June 22, 1944. Named after the Georgian military commander Pyotr Bagration, the operation aimed to destroy German Army Group Center and liberate Belarus, which had been under German occupation since 1941. The Russians launched it just after D-Day—the Allies' invasion of Northern France. It was also launched on the third anniversary of Operation Barbarossa—Hitler's invasion of Russia. Bagration was a disaster for Germany as Army Group Center was annihilated and the Russians advanced deep into Eastern Europe.

Bagration handed Germany its worst defeat in its history with over 400,000 casualties.

## Background

After the Soviet victories in the recent The Dnieper–Carpathian and Crimean offensives, they began probably the most lethal assault on Nazi Germany—Operation Bagration.

They had three options:

1. An assault on the Balkans and knock Romania and Bulgaria out of the Axis. This would also further threaten Nazi oil supply.
2. Focus on the north and into the Baltic States, splitting Army Groups North and Center.
3. An offensive in Belorussia against Germany's Army Group Center.

Option one would have driven the Soviets farther from their ultimate goal—Berlin. The planners also believed they were vulnerable to flanking and counter-attacks. Option two was judged as too ambitious. The Soviets chose Option three, as it would lead to Poland and ultimately Germany. They also agreed on a series of sequential offensives along the entire front, but the assault on Germany's Army Group Center was the linchpin of the operation. Crushing Army Group Center would cause the entire German front line to collapse.

At Bagration, the Soviets also employed a masterful application of the concept of deep battle. Instead of dividing the forces almost equally along the front, they focused on specific areas. Once the overwhelming force creates a gap in the German defenses, Soviet infantry and armor would rush in and exploit the opening. They would wreak havoc on both the enemy's flanks and rear. This change in tactic surprised the German command.

### Maskirovka

Another key to the Soviet victory was Maskirovka or Russian Military

Deception. In Bagration, they were able to reinforce German belief that the major attack would be on the South instead of the center. After the German defeat in The Dnieper–Carpathian and Crimean offensives earlier in 1944, the Germans believed that the area in front of Army Group South would be used as a staging area for a major Soviet offensive.

One reason this ruse worked was because the Soviets were indeed planning an attack on the South, though it wouldn't be the first, heaviest blow. As a result, the Germans moved the entire operational reserve on the Eastern Front to the South. They reduced Army Group Center's strength—one third of its artillery, half its tank destroyers, and 88% of its tanks.

Worse, because of Russia's deception strategy, the Germans underestimated Soviet infantry by 40%, mechanized forces by 300%, and the tanks and self-propelled guns as only 400 to 1800 instead of the 4,000 to 5,200.

Thus, even as the Soviet push to Belorussia intensified, German reserves in the South remained idle. This was similar to the US and UK's strategy for D-Day where they convinced the Germans that the main attacks were at the Pas de Calais. Weeks after D-Day and even when his forces at Normandy were in danger of annihilation, Hitler kept reserves at Pas de Calais for a phantom invasion that never came.

SCHEMES

*Figure 91.* A battery of Soviet heavy 203mm howitzers m1931, 3rd Belorussian front.

## Operation

To prepare for the attack, Belorussian partisans launched relentless assaults on the German supply lines, wreaking havoc with 10,000 explosions west of Minsk on June 19. The Soviets also initiated probing attacks to test enemy defenses.

The formal commencement of the operation began with an artillery bombardment, showcasing Russia's advancements in wartime production. They allocated each artillery piece six tons of ammunition for this crucial offensive.

Following the intense bombardment, the First Baltic and 3rd Belorussian Armies spearheaded the attack, with the goal of encircling Vitebsk. Tanks equipped with specially designed rollers advanced ahead, expertly detonating minefields, akin to the British flailing tanks which performed a similar task.

The following day, the Russians encircled Vitebsk, trapping the German 53rd Corps. Earlier Hitler rejected the corps' request to retreat. He later changed his mind, but by then it was too late. This would occur often during Operation Bagration.

Hitler's vacillations and refusal to allow his troops to withdraw to better defensive positions led to encirclement of hundreds of thousands of troops. He also came up with the concept of festungen or "fortress-cities," which were defended to the last man. By June 29, his fortress cities of Vitebsk, Orsha, Mogilev, and Bobruisk had fallen.

**Figure 92.** Soviet civilians, previously liberated from German concentration camps by the Red Army, return home near Vitebsk.

On June 23, the Russians launched twin attacks on the cities of Mogilev and Bobruisk. Marshal Konstantin Rokossovsky, one of the planners of Bagration, personally led the attack on Bobruisk. The massive bombardment was followed by waves of Ilyushin-2 Shturmovik "Flying Tank '' ground-attack aircraft that strafed and bombed the Germans.

On June 28, Mogilev fell. Bobruisk followed the next day.

After the two cities fell, the forces from Vitebsk and Bobruisk/Mogilev performed a pincer movement to encircle Mińsk.

Experienced German General Walter Model, known for his tactical brilliance with the policy of Shield and Sword, valiantly tried to salvage the dire situation during the advance of Operation Bagration. He was known as "The Fuhrer's Fireman" and deployed to salvage desperate situations. Despite requesting reinforcements from other Army groups, he could not prevent the encirclement and subsequent liberation of Minsk on July 3 and 4, respectively.

## OPERATION BAGRATION (SOVIET OFFENSIVE ON THE EASTERN FRONT)

*Figure 93.* A Panzer IV rushing to the front.

Meanwhile, Russian General Igor Bagramyan faced obstacles as well. While he wanted to rush towards Riga, the Stavka (Russia's High Command) insisted on capturing Šiauliai first. Eventually, Bagramyan received permission to push forward, reaching the Gulf of Riga on July 31, effectively separating Army Group North from the remnants of Army Group Center.

*Figure 94.* Polish Home Army (AK) and Soviet Soldiers in Wilno.

As the operation progressed, challenges such as unfavorable weather, supply issues, and German reinforcements from the Italian front slowed down Operation Bagration by mid-August. Nonetheless, the operation's initial momentum had already proven to be a significant blow to the German forces on the Eastern Front.

## *Warsaw Uprising*

On August 1, 1944, witnessing the steady advance of the Soviet Union, the Polish resistance movement started an uprising in their capital. Determined to liberate Warsaw independently, between 20,000 to 49,000 Poles took part in the revolt, even though only 2,500 of them possessed guns at the outset. With unparalleled bravery, they embarked on the largest military operation ever conducted by a European resistance group. Despite facing brutalities at the hands of the Nazis, including the tragic Wola massacre, the Poles persisted in their fight until finally surrendering on October 2.

As the uprising raged on, the city suffered destruction, with about 90% of it lying in ruins by the end. Tragically, many survivors were summarily executed or were sent to concentration camps.

The Poles expected a liberation similar to Paris when citizens supported by Allies freed the city. Unfortunately for the Poles, much of the expected help did not arrive. There were airdrops of supplies during the uprising, but these were not enough. These came from the RAF, South African Air Force, and the USAAF. The allies lost 41 planes while delivering 41 tons of supplies.

*Figure 95.* Warsaw Uprising. A Polish fighter from the Mokotów district, is coming out of sewers and surrendering to Germans. After the uprising, Nazi General Himmler ordered the city's destruction.

On July 24, the Soviets had captured the Polish city of Lublin, only 108 miles (172 km) from Warsaw. By July 28, the Soviets were only 25 miles (40 km) southeast of Warsaw. But even when the city was within artillery range, the Soviets refused to bombard the Germans.

The only outside help came from Polish General Zygmunt Berling's First Polish Army, a unit under the Soviet Belorussian Front. But they suffered heavy losses as they rushed to the city. According to some historians, Berling helped without the explicit approval of the Soviets. The failure of his assistance and his apparent insubordination allegedly caused his dismissal soon after.

Some claim that Stalin wanted the Germans to crush the uprising, while others claim it was a purely military decision as the Soviets prioritized bridgeheads for later advances. The Germans also mounted a stronger than expected defense.

The Warsaw Uprising had severe ramifications for the Poles. The Western Allies recognized the Polish government in exile in London, while the Soviets considered the new Lublin Committee as the executive governing authority. Many of the supporters of the government-in-exile were later arrested or killed.

## Aftermath

Operation Bagration was highly successful and resulted in a decisive victory for the Soviet Union. The German Army Group Center was virtually annihilated, with the Soviet forces inflicting heavy casualties and capturing or destroying large numbers of German tanks, artillery, and vehicles.

In five weeks, the Red Army had advanced over 340 miles (550 km) and was knocking on Warsaw's door. They annihilated Army Group Center. Germany never recovered from this defeat.

Soon after Bagration, there was more bad news for Germany as its two allies, Romania and Hungary defected to the Soviet side.

**Figure 96.** The Russians paraded 57,000 German prisoners-of-war in Moscow on July 17, 1944.

# Operation Market Garden (Allied Airborne Operation in the Netherlands)

*September 17 to 27, 1844*

**Belligerents:** British, American, Polish, Canadian, Belgian, Dutch forces vs. Germany

**Objective:** Outflank the German defenses on the Siegfried Line by capturing bridges over the rivers Meuse, Waal, and Rhine.

**Outcome:** Allies failed to capture the critical bridge at Arnhem. About one-fifth of the Netherlands was liberated, including Eindhoven and Nijmegen. Indirectly resulted in the Dutch famine of 1944.

Operation Market Garden was a large-scale Allied military operation during World War II. It was launched in September 1944 to secure key bridges in the Netherlands and cross the Rhine River, allowing the Allies to advance into Germany and potentially bring a swift end to the war.

Field Marshal Bernard Montgomery, the British commander of the 21st Army Group planned the operation. It involved a combined airborne and ground assault. The airborne component, code-named Operation Market, consisted of three divisions dropped behind enemy lines to secure bridgeheads along the route from the Netherlands to Arnhem. The ground component, Operation Garden, involved armored and infantry units moving rapidly to link up with the airborne forces.

The operation was ambitious and relied on a rapid advance through the Netherlands, crossing multiple major rivers and capturing key bridges intact.

The ultimate aim was to secure a bridgehead over the Rhine at Arnhem, cutting off German forces and facilitating the push into Germany.

The operation became one of the most controversial campaigns of the Second World War.

**Figure 97.** Men of the 2nd Battalion South Staffordshire Regiment entering Oosterbeek along the Utrechtsweg on their way towards Arnhem, 18 September 1944.

## Background

After the breakout at Normandy, the Allies wanted to keep the pressure on the Germans. Dwight Eisenhower wanted to adopt a broad front strategy, attacking the Germans simultaneously on several fronts. Unfortunately for the Allies, their supply problem, especially fuel, precluded this approach. At this point they consumed five gallons of fuel to deliver one gallon to the front. This was unsustainable, and they needed alternatives before they could launch another major operation.

British general Bernard Montgomery thought he had a solution. Operation Market Garden was born.

## Operation

Montgomery proposed cutting through the Netherlands and getting a foothold across the Rhine. This involved seizing strategic bridges along the way using airborne troops (Market) while armor and more infantry linked up with them (Garden). Market was under the command of British Lieutenant General Frederick Browning while Garden was under Lieutenant General Brian Horrocks, also British.

As Supreme Commander of the Allied Expeditionary Force, Dwight Eisenhower had overall command.

On paper, the plan was simple. Three airborne divisions landed at or near various bridges in the Netherlands. The units were:

1. 101st US Airborne—at Eindhoven, to capture the bridges at Son and Veghel
2. 82nd Us Airborne—at Nijmegen, to capture the Grave and Nijmegen bridges
3. 1st British Airborne, later complemented by the Polish First parachute Brigade—the road and rail bridges at Arnhem.

Upon capturing Arnhem, another unit was supposed to land at the nearby Deelen airfield. The paratroopers needed to hold these objectives until armor and infantry relieved them.

Given the breakthroughs in France, the Allies believed the German armies in the Netherlands were on the verge of collapse. What they didn't know was that parts of two Panzer divisions were in the area to rest and refit. This piece of intelligence was relayed to Allied High Command, but was largely ignored. The planners believed the aerial photographs were not conclusive enough. Worse, at that point, there was also a suspicion that the Dutch Resistance had been compromised.

One other issue was the lack of transport planes, which resulted in the landings happening in three batches. Despite misgivings, however, the Allies believed the risk was worth it and proceeded.

The US airborne troops landed at or near their objectives while the British landed a few miles away from Arnhem Bridge. This proved critical as only one battalion, led by Lt. Colonel John Frost captured the northern end of the bridge while the rest guarded the drop zone near Oosterbeek. Unfortunately for the paratroopers, the Germans on the other side of the bridge had range weapons—artillery, rockets, and mortars that outranged and outgunned the British.

At Nijmegen, the 82nd Airborne easily captured Grave Bridge, but not the longer Nijmegen Bridge. US General James Gavin positioned his troops to defend against a German counter-attack. They successfully repelled the attack, but it delayed their capture of the strategic bridge. This delay had major repercussions.

At Eindhoven, the 101st the airborne units captured the Veghel bridge, although the Germans blew up Son bridge. On the 3rd day of the operation the armored units finally linked up with the paratroopers. Engineers built a replacement Bailey bridge for Son and the armored units advanced to Nijmegen.

*Figure 98.* Dutch civilians offer drinks to the crew of a Cromwell tank of 2nd Welsh Guards during the liberation of Eindhoven, 19 September 1944.

As the tanks reached Nijmegen, they discovered that the bridge remained in German hands. And even though the bridge was captured shortly, the area near Nijmegen had to be cleared before armor could advance. This and German counter attacks from the forest further delayed the 30th Armor division's advance.

**Figure 99.** Tanks from the British Second Army roll over the Nijmegen Waal Bridge.

During the Arnhem and Oosterbeek operations, the British troops faced severe shortages and relied on air dropped supplies from the Allies. Unfortunately, the Germans intercepted much of the supplies. Days later, the arrival of the Polish brigade brought a much-needed respite to the British forces, as they swiftly reinforced the 1st British airborne in Oosterbeek and played a crucial role in repelling multiple German counter-attacks. The weather and lack of transport planes had delayed the Poles.

**Figure 100.** British airborne forces using a 6-pounder anti-tank gun at Arnhem.

Meanwhile, John Frost's men had completely run out of ammunition and hundreds needed immediate medical care. With no means to fight back, he surrendered on September 21. When the Germans regained control of Arnhem Bridge, the counter-attacks became more intense.

When Arnhem fell to complete German control, and with two-thirds casualties, the British and Polish withdrew.

Operation Market Garden was over.

## Aftermath

Operation Market Garden was a strategic setback for the Allies. While some ground was gained and bridges were captured, failing to secure the crucial bridge at Arnhem prevented the rapid advance into Germany. The operation resulted in significant casualties, particularly among the British 1st Airborne Division.

The casualties were not limited to the soldiers. One unintended result of the operation was the Dutch famine of 1944. Dutch supporters sabotaged railways and German operations to support the liberation, much like what the French did a few months earlier. The Germans responded with an embargo on food and over 18,000 Dutch civilians died.

Despite this, the Allies had liberated about a fifth of the Netherlands and the Allies consolidated their gains. Operation Pheasant, conducted a month later, liberated even more of the Netherlands. However, the country wouldn't be completely free until the German surrender in May 1945.

In a final ironic twist to Market Garden, and in a bid to stop the repeated German counterattacks, the Allies bombed and destroyed Arnhem Bridge.

# Operation Bodenplatte (The Luftwaffe's Last Stand)

*January 1, 1945*

*Belligerents:* Germany vs. Allies

*Objective:* Destroy Allied Airpower and restore the initiative to the Germans in the Battle of the Bulge

*Outcome:* Luftwaffe eliminated as a major fighting force.

Operation Bodenplatte was the Luftwaffe's last major offensive. It was originally planned to support Hitler's Ardennes Offensive, but the same weather that grounded the allies also stopped the Luftwaffe from taking to the air.

## Background

By late December, Hitler's Ardennes offensive better known as the Battle of the Bulge, had ground to a halt. In a desperate attempt to reclaim the initiative, Hitler approved two operations: Operation Northwind for his land forces and Operation Bodenplatte.

Bodenplatte's aim was to cripple the air forces scattered in the Low Countries and thus gain air superiority in the Ardennes area and beyond. In an ironic twist, the pilots would be attacking air bases which they once called home just months earlier.

Some German commanders, notably General der Jagdflieger Adolf Galland, protested against the operation, arguing that the last reserves of the Luftwaffe should defend Germany against strategic bombing. However, Luftwaffe chief Hermann Göring was adamant to launch the operation. His prestige had taken a hit, and he needed a victory. Soon, every fighter and fighter-bomber unit in the Western front was involved in the attack.

## Operation

The operation was unique as each squadron had at least one ME-262 jet fighter. However, these jets did not take part in the attack and were assigned to monitor the performance of the attacking Luftwaffe pilots.

The forces were to attack 17 separate targets in the Netherlands, Belgium, Luxembourg, and France. They expected complete surprise and because it was New Year's Day, they also expected the Allies to have a hangover and mount lighter defenses.

The operation began badly. To preserve secrecy, the Luftwaffe had not advised the air defenses about the operation early enough. Thus the Luftwaffe suffered casualties from German flak, especially as they passed by the V2 launch sites. They lost 16 planes to friendly fire before they even left Germany.

There were, however, some successes in the early moments of the attack. About half of the target airfields suffered moderate or severe casualties. The worst hit were the airfields in Belgium (Three in Brussels, and one each from Maldegem, Sint-Truiden, and Ghent), with 124 planes destroyed and at least 71 damaged. Also badly hit was an airfield in Eindhoven, Netherlands where 41 planes were destroyed.

*Figure 101.* P-47 Lightnings destroyed at the Metz Airfield during Operation Bodenplatte.

The mission was supposed to be a strafe and run attack, but many inexperienced pilots of the Luftwaffe lingered at the airfield, making themselves vulnerable to flak and counter-attack. Planes returning from patrol or were able to launch soon shot down the German planes.

**Figure 102.** Fire crews cover an Avro Lancaster with foam to save it from burning, at B58/Melsbroek, Belgium, following the attack on the airfield by Luftwaffe fighter-bombers.

When they returned to base, they flew slower as they tried to maintain formation. Seeing this, the Luftwaffe leaders ordered them to break into two-man teams and escape to Germany. Unfortunately, once they reached Germany, they were once more attacked with friendly fire from the air defenses.

## Aftermath

The Germans achieved tactical and short-term success. They had destroyed about 305 allied aircraft and damaged 190 others. Allied pilot losses were light as most of the planes were destroyed on the ground. On the other hand, the Luftwaffe lost 271 fighters and 9 Ju-88s, along with 89 damaged aircraft. Worse for the Luftwaffe was the loss of 213 pilots, about a third of whom were experienced. The Allies could replace their losses, but the Luftwaffe could not.

*Figure 103.* Fire crews attempt to extinguish the last fires among burnt-out North American Mitchells at B58/Melsbroek, Belgium.

Operation Bodenplatte was ultimately the last hurrah of the Luftwaffe.

# Operation Varsity (Allied Airborne Assault on Germany, Part of Operation Plunder)

***March 24, 1945***

**Belligerents:** United Kingdom, United States, and Canada vs. Germany

**Objective:** Support the amphibious troops as part of Operation Plunder

**Outcome:** Airborne troops captured all objectives, though with huge casualties.

Operation Varsity was the last major, successful Allied airborne operation in World War 2. It involved over 16,000 paratroopers and was part of the final push to enter Northern Germany. Varsity was also the largest airborne operation in history to be conducted in one day and in one location. Operation Overlord had 20,000 paratroopers, but they were split into two distinct areas. Market Garden had 34,000 airborne troops, but they were dispersed into several areas and dropped in batches. Varsity involved over 1,600 transports, 1,300 gliders and almost 900 fighters to support the airdrop.

In contrast to D-Day, the paratroopers in this operation executed their landings after the amphibious units started the assault. Despite the risks of daylight landings, they aimed to minimize dispersion and focused on capturing strategic defensive positions near Hamminkeln and Weasel, both situated deep behind enemy lines. Their crucial mission involved seizing key roads and bridges to safeguard against immediate counter-attacks and enable the safe passage of the rest of the assault troops crossing the Rhine

River.

## Background

The River Rhine had always protected Germany—a natural barrier that was impossible to cross for anyone but the greatest generals. Caesar famously crossed it in 56 BC, using a bridge his engineers built in only ten days. The French armies made another crossing in 1797 under Napoleon—the last in almost 150 years.

And so after crossing the Siegfried Line in 1945 the Allies armies faced the same obstacle as Caesar and Napoleon. In response, British General Bernard Montgomery crafted Operation Plunder and its major component, Operation Varsity. Montgomery planned to let his 21st Army Group cross the Rhine at the town of Rees, in the state of North Rhine-Westphalia, Germany. The British Second Army and the US Ninth Army were to cross just south of the river Lippe, parts of which run along the Ruhr area.

But weeks before the start date of Montgomery's meticulously planned assault, elements of the US Ninth Armored Division captured the bridge at Remagen, and the unit became the first to cross the Rhine in number.

And to Montgomery's chagrin, on March 22 US General George Patton and his Third Army also crossed the river near Oppenheim. Like in Sicily, Patton beat his old British rival in the race to capture a strategic objective.

## Operation

On the evening of March 23, four thousand guns bombarded the German positions and by the early hours of March 24, the amphibious infantry had secured several crossings at the Rhine. Eisenhower's fear that elite German troops would hinder the landings proved mostly unfounded.

**Figure 104.** Douglas Dakotas fly in formation over Wavre, Belgium, heading for the dropping zones east of the River Rhine. Above them, Dakotas towing Airspeed Horsas fly a divergent course towards their objectives.

Thirteen hours after the ground assault began, the paratroopers landed. Over 9,000 American and 7,000 British and Canadian troops were transported by varying transports and gliders and protected by fighters. Most were dropped at the correct drop zones, though the daytime landings meant they met more anti-aircraft fire.

The British and Canadians immediately met their key objectives, including the capture of Schnappenberg, Schermbeck, Hamminkeln, and Diersfordt.

The troops suffered over 2,400 casualties.

## Aftermath

Along with the capture of the Ludendorff Bridge at Remagen, the crossing of Patton's 3rd Army, Operations Plunder and Varsity the fall of Nazi Germany was just a matter of time.

**Figure 105.** British airborne troops with a 6-pdr anti-tank gun in Hamminkeln, Germany, 25 March 1945.

Some historians have questioned the need for Operation Varsity. They pointed out that unlike D-Day, there was no "Atlantic Wall" on the Rhine. Moreover, the paratroopers landed after the assault began, meaning the amphibious troops could've captured the objectives with less casualties. The airdrops were also done in daylight, where the airborne forces were more susceptible to anti-aircraft fire and capture.

Still, General Eisenhower called it "the most successful airborne operation carried out to date." It captured all of its major objectives, destroyed enemy defenses, and in the first hours, protected the landing troops against a major counterattack.

*Figure 106.* Airborne troops study a sign outside Hamminkeln during operations east of the Rhine, 25 March 1945.

Operation Varsity marked a significant achievement for the Allied forces, as it played a crucial role in breaching the formidable natural barrier of the Rhine and facilitating the final push into Germany. The success of the operation further weakened German defenses and contributed to the eventual collapse of the Nazi regime.

# Operation Amherst (Airdrop of Mainly French Commandos in the Netherlands)

**April 7 to 8, 1945**

**Belligerents:** France, assisted by the United Kingdom, Canada, Belgium, and Poland vs. Germany

**Objectives:** Capture bridges, canals, and airfields intact in the Netherlands. Sow confusion among the German defenders.

**Outcome:** All objectives met.

Operation Amherst was a military operation conducted by the Allied forces during World War II. It took place on March 7-12, 1945, and was part of the larger Allied effort to liberate the Netherlands from German occupation.

The objective of Operation Amherst was to sow confusion among the German defenders, and to secure key bridges, canals, and other structures in the Dutch province of Drenthe. The Special Air Service (SAS), which by this time included both French and British units, executed the operation. Members of the Dutch resistance assisted them and later by the 2nd Canadian Army Corps, which was advancing from Nijmegen and Arnhem. The Canadians will then proceed to the North Sea.

## Background

By April 1945, although the war was going badly for the Germans, they continued to resist fiercely. Like in their retreats from the Italian and Eastern fronts, they destroyed cities and infrastructure. To counter this, the Allies came up with Operation Amherst, with the aim of capturing 22 objectives: 18 canal and river bridges, and 4 airfields.

Tasked with implementing Operation Amherst were a group of commandos composed of mainly French elite special forces. They were to parachute into the Netherlands and hold on to their objectives until a Canadian army could relieve them.

## Operation

In the afternoon of April 7, the Frenchmen were driven to the designated airfields. A special unit joined them, tasked with organizing Dutch resistance in the area. This special unit was composed of two Englishmen and two Dutch officers.

**Figure 107.** A Short Stirling bomber, similar to the one used to deliver troops in Operation Amherst.

At around 9pm, 46 four-engine planes took off from Southeast England. Operation Amherst had begun and in a few hours, some 700 French Special Air Service paratroopers and other soldiers, all under the command of British general Mike Calvert would drop around Drenthe in the Netherlands.

The airdrop was difficult. The paratroopers were dropped at an altitude of between 1,500 and 2,000 feet, meaning their parachute descent lasted nearly two minutes. There were also strong winds of 13.5 knots or 25 km/h, which also accounted for the dispersed landings.

But although the paratroopers were widely dispersed, they soon captured all of their objectives. When they captured the small airfield at Havelte, however, they found out that there were large craters caused by a bombing run by the Americans.

Other Allied foreign units operating in the area supported the French commandos. Belgian units used their jeeps to transport the wounded. A Polish reconnaissance team also assisted the French in seizing their objectives, especially at Westerbork.

Their success was tempered by retaliatory actions from the Nazis, who massacred at least 15 Dutch civilians at the hamlet of Spier in the municipality of Midden-Drenthe. The Germans also executed 7 captured paratroopers.

## Aftermath

The operation was a success, and the Canadians were soon moving towards the North Sea. Some bridges were wired, but the French were able to stop the demolition. It was a moment of triumph for the French soldiers.

Charles de Gaulle, leader of the Free French later said, "Eux regardent le ciel sans pâlir et la terre sans rougir" (They look at the sky without going pale and look at the ground without shame).

# Operation Ten-Go (The Battleship Yamato's Last Stand)

**April 7, 1945**

    **Belligerents:** Japan vs. the United States

    **Objectives:** Support troops in the Battle of Okinawa. Beach Yamato and use the battleship as a fixed shore battery

    **Outcome:** Yamato sinks before reaching Okinawa

Operation Ten-Go or Operation Heaven One was the last major Japanese naval operation in World War 2. It was part of the larger Battle of Okinawa.

Even without air cover, the legendary battleship Yamato led the attack. The Yamato and her sister ship, the Musashi, were the heaviest and most powerful battleships ever built.

## Background

After crippling losses at the Solomons and the Philippines, the Imperial Japanese Navy, once the behemoth of the Pacific, was no longer as formidable. Their ships no longer dared venture out of the open because of American air superiority in the theater.

On April 1, 1945 elements of the Army's XXIV Corps landed on the beaches of

Okinawa as the main elements in the landing force.

In order to defend the island, the Japanese Army declared they would use their air force and launch Kamikaze. The Emperor then asked, "Where's the Navy?" The Navy's top brass, feeling the pressure, launched a Kamikaze-style attack using the Yamato. Other officials felt that risking a symbol of Japanese might to be wasteful, especially since they didn't expect the ship to survive. They felt the Yamato was better used defending the main islands. But the series of Japanese defeats and mounting criticism that the Yamato had been reduced to nothing more than a hotel for the Navy's top officials sealed the ship's fate.

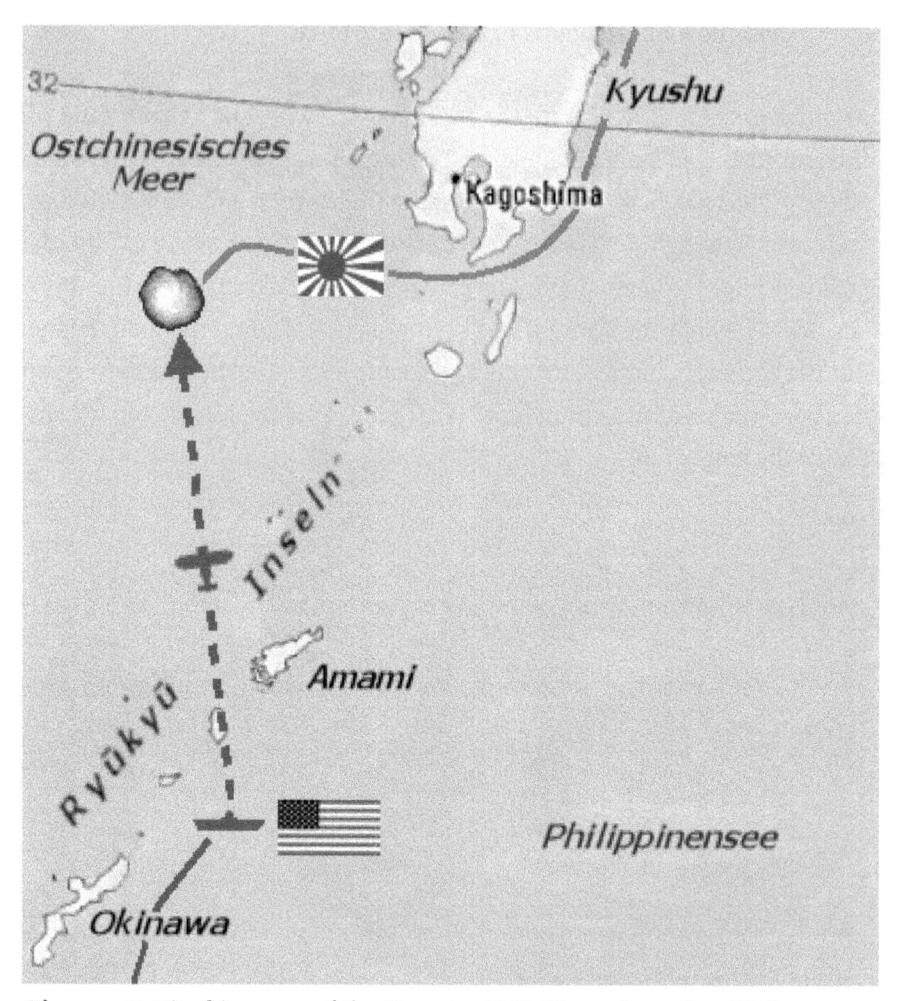

**Figure 108.** Final journey of the Yamato. Solid lines show the ship's course. Dotted lines show the route of the American fleet.

## Operation

The Japanese hoped they could sail to Okinawa undetected, but the decryption of Japanese messages made that impossible.

The Yamato sailed on April 6 and the following day, American planes appeared on the horizon. American Hellcat and Corsair fighters conducted a fighter sweep, and were surprised there was no air cover. The battleship's only protection were its over 150 anti-aircraft guns and a screening force of one light cruiser and eight destroyers.

*Figure 109.* The Japanese battleship Yamato under attack by U.S. Navy carrier aircraft on 7 April 1945, as a bomb explodes off its port side. The fire in the area of the aft 155mm turret can be clearly seen.

Dive bombers were free to attack at will, while Torpedo planes were advised to only attack on one side to prevent effective counter-flooding.

The Yamato performed evasive maneuvers, but at least 11 torpedoes and 2 armor-piercing bombs hit her. At just after 2pm, the giant battleship began to sink.

*Figure 110.* Smoke rises to the clouds shortly after the Japanese battleship Yamato capsized, exploded and sank.

## Aftermath

Some historians compare the sinking of the Yamato to that of the Prince of Wales in December 1941. Both were prides of their navies and both were sunk by naval air power.

After Operation Ten-go, the Japanese Navy was essentially destroyed.

# Notable Canceled Operations

## Operation Sea Lion (Unternehmen Seelöwe or The Nazi Planned Invasion of the British Isles)

**1940**

    **Objective**: Amphibious Invasion of the British Isles

    **Outcome**: Canceled after the Battle of Britain, where the Luftwaffe failed to gain air superiority

Operation Sea Lion, also known as Unternehmen Seelöwe in German, was Nazi Germany's ambitious plan to invade the United Kingdom during World War II. After the British refused to accept terms to end the war, Adolf Hitler and the German high command considered a large-scale amphibious assault across the English Channel as the next step to conquer Britain.

The plan for Operation Sea Lion involved a coordinated attack by German air, land, and naval forces, aiming to establish a foothold in southern England and subsequently advance across the country.

Following the Fall of France in June 1940, the Nazis saw the potential invasion and occupation of the British Isles as a strategic opportunity to bring the UK to its knees and secure their position in Europe. However, logistical challenges, the Royal Navy's resistance, and the British resolve to defend their homeland ultimately led to the postponement and eventual

## NOTABLE CANCELED OPERATIONS

cancellation of the ambitious Operation Sea Lion.

Success hinged on the Luftwaffe gaining air superiority over the RAF. However, the Battle of Britain, spanning from July to October 1940, marked a critical turning point. The RAF successfully fended off the Luftwaffe's attacks and maintained control of the skies.

Hitler's decision to divert forces to other fronts in October 1940, along with failing to convince the British of an imminent invasion, further diminished the threat. With the launch of Operation Barbarossa in June 1941, the focus shifted entirely, and the possibility of a large-scale invasion no longer loomed over the United Kingdom.

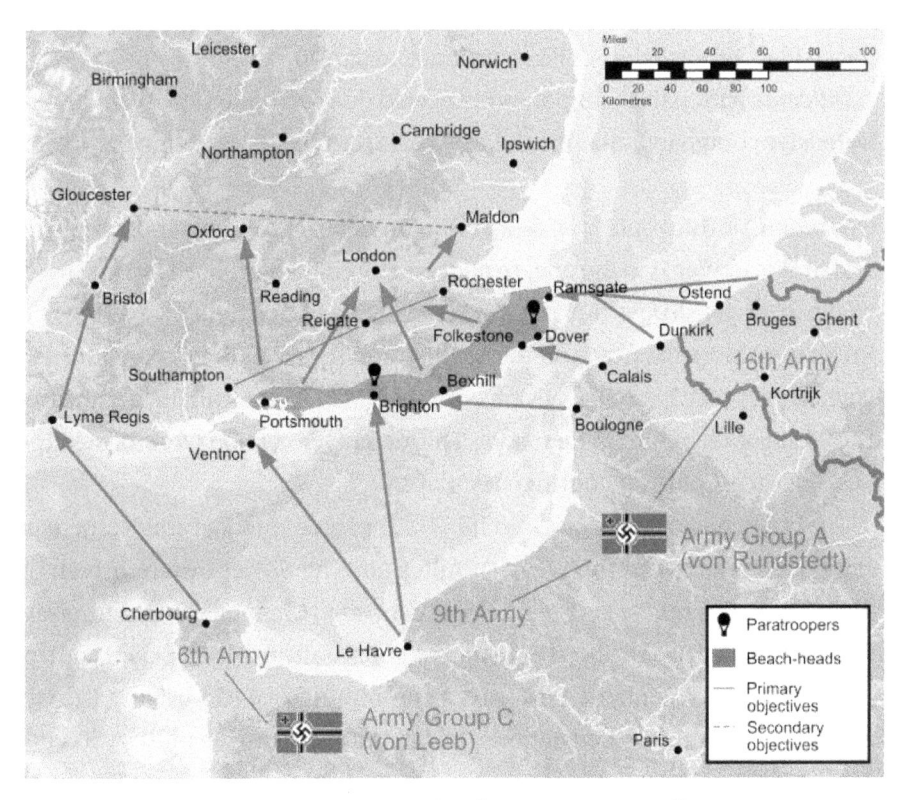

*Figure 111.* Invasion plan for Operation Sealion.

One retrospective view is that even if the Germans won the Battle of Britain, they still had to contend with the formidable Royal Navy. Plus British aircraft production had also increased, challenging the Luftwaffe's air superiority. Thus some historians believe that Operation Sealion had no chance to succeed.

## Operation Unthinkable (British Plans for a Potential Post World War 2 Conflict with the Soviet Union)

**1945**

*Objective:* (Offensive) Surprise Attack on the Soviets, (Defensive) Contingency Plans in case the Soviets continued expansion

*Outcome:* Offensive component canceled due to impracticality and risks. Defensive component became the first basis for Cold War contingency plans.

Operation Unthinkable was a British plan devised in 1945, following the end of World War II in Europe, to address the challenge posed by the Soviet Union after defeating the Nazis. The plan had two variations: one offensive, involving a surprise attack on the Soviets, and the other defensive, aimed at countering potential Soviet advances to the North Sea or Atlantic Ocean after the withdrawal of American forces. This defensive version later formed the basis of early Cold War contingency plans.

The brainchild of Winston Churchill, Unthinkable emerged amidst increasing tensions between the Western Allies and the Soviet Union, driven by ideological differences and geopolitical concerns. Churchill sought to assert Allied influence over Eastern Europe and potentially roll back Soviet control in the region. The plan envisioned a combined force comprising British, American, and other Allied nations, launching a large-scale military assault against the Soviet Union.

However, Operation Unthinkable was ultimately deemed impractical and highly risky. The Soviets had a numerical superiority of about 2:1 in manpower. At the time the Americans were also preparing for a possible invasion of Japan. They couldn't and wouldn't commit forces.

This operation was deemed catastrophic for everyone involved. And except for the defensive provisions in the second version, Operation Unthinkable was canceled completely.

While Operation Unthinkable itself did not materialize, it serves as a historical example of the complex dynamics and strategic considerations during the immediate post-war period.

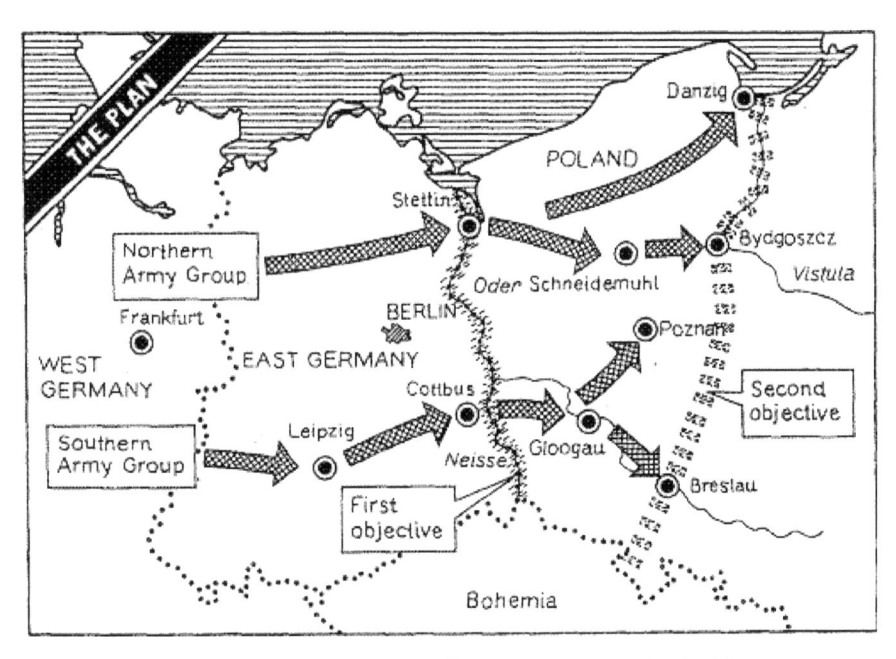

*Figure 112.* Plan of Attack for Operation Unthinkable.

## Operation Downfall (Planned Invasion of Japan by the Allies)

**1945**
  *Objective:* Amphibious and Airborne Invasion of Japan
  *Outcome:* Canceled as Japan surrendered after the two atomic bombs.

Operation Downfall was the proposed Allied plan for the invasion of Japan during World War II. It comprised two major operations: Operation Olympic and Operation Coronet. The plan was developed in 1945 as the Allies prepared for the potential invasion of the Japanese mainland.

Operation Olympic was the first phase of the plan and involved a massive amphibious assault on the southernmost Japanese island of Kyushu. The goal was to establish a foothold and secure airfields for subsequent operations. It was scheduled to begin in November 1945.

Operation Coronet was the second phase and aimed to invade the main island of Honshu near Tokyo. It was a larger and more ambitious operation involving multiple landings on the Tokyo Plain. The objective was to defeat the remaining Japanese forces and capture the capital city.

The planned invasion of Japan was expected to be a formidable and costly undertaking. Japanese soldiers had shown their determination to fight to the last man, and Allied leaders expected heavy casualties on both sides. The estimated casualty figures for the Allied forces ranged from several hundred thousands to more than a million.

However, Operation Downfall never came to fruition. The dropping of atomic bombs on the Japanese cities of Hiroshima and Nagasaki in August 1945, combined with the Soviet Union's declaration of war on Japan, led to Japan's surrender. The bombings prompted Emperor Hirohito to accept the terms of the Potsdam Declaration, effectively ending World War II.

# NOTABLE CANCELED OPERATIONS

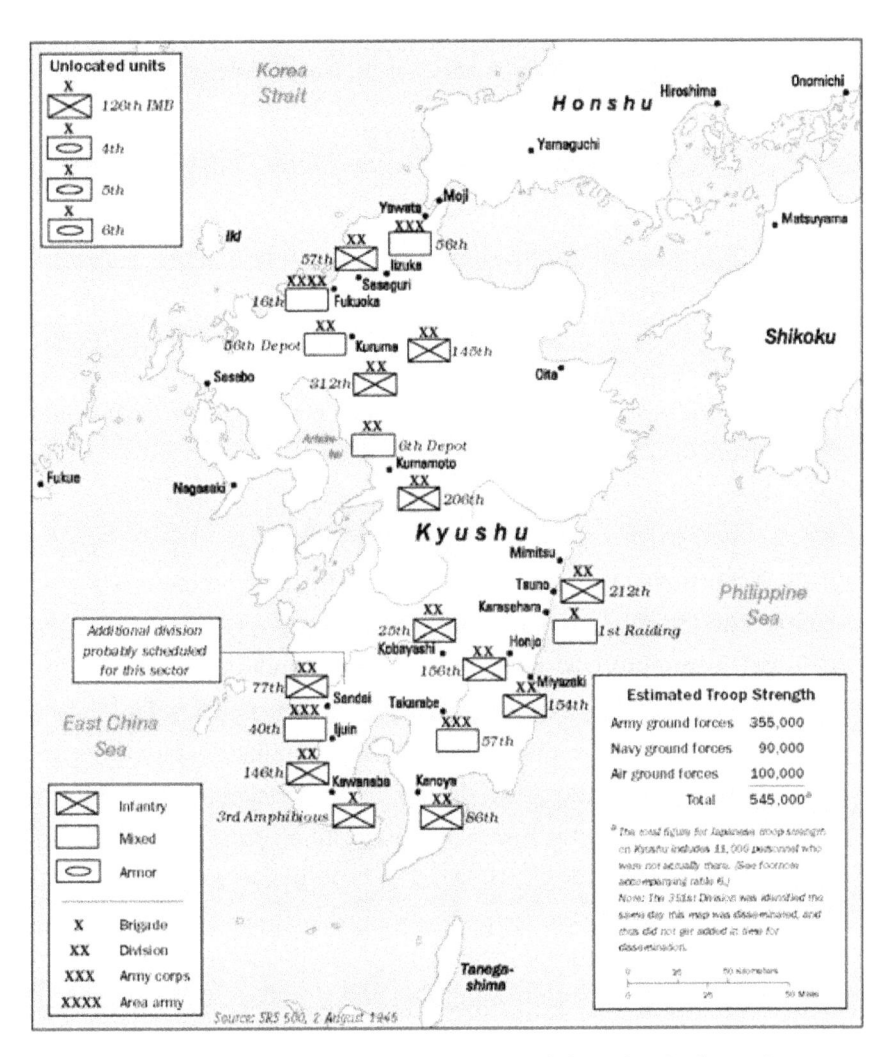

**Figure 113.** Estimated troops for the invasion of the Island of Kyushu as part of Operation Downfall.

# Images

*All images in this book are either in the public domain or published under a Creative Commons copyright license. The numbers represent the images' appearance in the book followed by the source. In some cases, the original captions were retained.*

1. By Dymetrios - Own work, CC BY-SA 4.0, https://commons.wikimedia.org/w/index.php?curid=106115673
2. https://commons.wikimedia.org/wiki/File:Bundesarchiv_Bild_101I-382-0248-33A,_Im_Westen,_Panzer_II_und_Panzer_I.jpg
3. By Strait_of_Dover_map.png: User:NormanEinsteinderivative work: Diannaa - This file was derived from: Strait of Dover map.png:Information on shipping routes from Thompson, Julian (2011) [2008]. Dunkirk: Retreat to Victory. New York: Arcade. ISBN 978-1-61145-314-0. Map, page 223., CC BY-SA 3.0, https://commons.wikimedia.org/w/index.php?curid=28440418
4. By Unknown author - http://media.iwm.org.uk/iwm/mediaLib//14/media-14092/large.jpgThis photograph HU 1145 comes from the collections of the Imperial War Museums., Public Domain, https://commons.wikimedia.org/w/index.php?curid=25297540
5. By derivative work: Maxrossomachin - This SVG map includes elements from this map:, CC BY-SA 3.0, https://commons.wikimedia.org/w/index.php?curid=31923321
6. By Jacques Mulard - Phototèque personnelle de l&#039;auteur, CC BY-SA 3.0, https://commons.wikimedia.org/w/index.php?curid=3914615
7. By Unknown author - my militar photo, CC BY-SA 4.0, https://common

## IMAGES

s.wikimedia.org/w/index.php?curid=66799294

8. By Cassowary Colorizations - Colonel-General Erwin Rommel helping to move his Škoda Superb Kfz 21 car, which had gotten stuck in the desert sand, as General Siegfried Westphal looks behind, 1941, CC BY 2.0, https://commons.wikimedia.org/w/index.php?curid=97710414

9. By Bundesarchiv, Bild 101I-782-0023-09A / Moosmüller / CC-BY-SA 3.0, CC BY-SA 3.0 de, https://commons.wikimedia.org/w/index.php?curid=5477785

10. By Bundesarchiv, Bild 146-1973-035-12 / CC-BY-SA 3.0, CC BY-SA 3.0 de, https://commons.wikimedia.org/w/index.php?curid=18498634

11. By DIREKTOR (derived from PANONIAN&#039;s work) - Own work using:File:Fascist_occupation_of_yugoslavia.pngData: Tomasevich, Jozo (1975) "Map 3: Partition of 1941" in War and Revolution in Yugoslavia, 1941–1945: The Chetniks, Stanford: Stanford University Press, p. 90 ISBN: 0-8047-0857-6. OCLC: 1203356. &lt;/ref&gt;, Public Domain, https://commons.wikimedia.org/w/index.php?curid=15371583

12. By Imperial Japanese Navy - Official U.S. Navy photograph NH 50930., Public Domain, https://commons.wikimedia.org/w/index.php?curid=223876

13. By Photographer: UnknownRetouched by: Mmxx - This tag does not indicate the copyright status of the attached work. A normal copyright tag is still required. See Commons:Licensing., Public Domain, https://commons.wikimedia.org/w/index.php?curid=18147474

14. By Unknown navy photographer - US archives, Public Domain, https://commons.wikimedia.org/w/index.php?curid=3008018

15. By U.S. Navy, Office of Public Relations - This tag does not indicate the copyright status of the attached work. A normal copyright tag is still required. See Commons:Licensing., Public Domain, https://commons.wikimedia.org/w/index.php?curid=16334170

16. By Unknown author U.S. Navy (photo 80-G-43376) - This tag does not indicate the copyright status of the attached work. A normal copyright tag is still required. See Commons:Licensing., Public Domain, https://c

ommons.wikimedia.org/w/index.php?curid=482800
17. By U.S. Navy, Photographed from a Naval Air Station Key West aircraft; The original uploader was Tannin at English Wikipedia. 2004-04-05 (original upload date) - This image is available from the United States Library of Congress&#039;s Prints and Photographs division under the digital ID fsa.8e01531.This tag does not indicate the copyright status of the attached work. A normal copyright tag is still required. See Commons:Licensing., Public Domain, https://commons.wikimedia.org/w/index.php?curid=3614491
18. By RAAF - Royal Australian Air Force 1939–1942, Public Domain, https://commons.wikimedia.org/w/index.php?curid=6872008
19. By © Sémhur / Wikimedia Commons, CC BY-SA 4.0, https://commons.wikimedia.org/w/index.php?curid=2357823
20. By Bundesarchiv, Bild 101II-MW-3722-03 / Kramer / CC-BY-SA 3.0, CC BY-SA 3.0 de, https://commons.wikimedia.org/w/index.php?curid=5478466
21. By Unknown author - This image was provided to Wikimedia Commons by the German Federal Archive (Deutsches Bundesarchiv) as part of a cooperation project. The German Federal Archive guarantees an authentic representation only using the originals (negative and/or positive), resp. the digitalization of the originals as provided by the Digital Image Archive., Public Domain, https://commons.wikimedia.org/w/index.php?curid=5418925
22. By jockrutherford from Owen Sound, ON - Operation Anthropoid, CC BY-SA 2.0, https://commons.wikimedia.org/w/index.php?curid=65272402
23. By Japanese military - U.S. Navy National Museum of Naval Aviation photo No. 1996.488.037.009; US Navy photo NH 73059., Public Domain, https://commons.wikimedia.org/w/index.php?curid=1509441
24. By Unknown author - U.S. Navy photo 80-G-16651, Public Domain, https://commons.wikimedia.org/w/index.php?curid=2900677
25. By Unknown author - U.S. Navy photo 80-G-451086, Public Domain, https://commons.wikimedia.org/w/index.php?curid=932592
26. By U.S. Navy - Official U.S. Navy photo 80-G-66121 from the U.S. Naval

History and Heritage Command. Transferred from en.wikipedia to Commons., 12 November 2006 (original upload date); 23 June 2011 (last version), Public Domain, https://commons.wikimedia.org/w/index.php?curid=15592626

27. By National Museum of the U.S. Navy - Battle of Midway, June 1942, Public Domain, https://commons.wikimedia.org/w/index.php?curid=70726568

28. By USN - U.S. Navy Naval History and Heritage Command photo 80-G-32301, Public Domain, https://commons.wikimedia.org/w/index.php?curid=49981

29. By Scouting Squadron 8 (VS-8), U.S. Navy; The original uploader was Palm dogg at English Wikipedia., 2006-01-30 (first version); 2006-02-14 (last version) - Official U.S. Navy photo 80-G-17054 from the U.S. Naval History and Heritage Command; originally from en.wikipedia; description page is/was here., Public Domain, https://commons.wikimedia.org/w/index.php?curid=2062084

30. By Not mentioned. Probably a German soldier. - English Wikipedia, Public Domain, https://commons.wikimedia.org/w/index.php?curid=3057336

31. By Fotoafdrukken Koninklijke Landmacht - https://nimh-beeldbank.defensie.nl/foto-s/detail/58ce8050-eb18-11df-a391-13966e870614/media/5e6f5dd8-5b8b-f2e6-e1b9-913b8d16a97b, CC0, https://commons.wikimedia.org/w/index.php?curid=131254587

32. By The Why We Fight series was created by the US Army Pictorial Services; Maps were prepared by the US War Department. - Screenshot taken from The Battle of Russia., Public Domain, https://commons.wikimedia.org/w/index.php?curid=6664860

33. By Schneider - https://audiovis.nac.gov.pl/obraz/1906/, Public Domain, https://commons.wikimedia.org/w/index.php?curid=79566095

34. By Hahle - https://audiovis.nac.gov.pl/obraz/2738/, Public Domain, https://commons.wikimedia.org/w/index.php?curid=79567173

35. https://commons.wikimedia.org/wiki/File:Einsatzgruppen_murder_Jews_in_Ivanhorod,_Ukraine,_1942.jpg

SCHEMES

36. By Pelman, L (Lt), Royal Navy official photographer - http://media.iwm.org.uk/iwm/mediaLib//29/media-29542/large.jpgThis photograph A 11223 comes from the collections of the Imperial War Museums., Public Domain, https://commons.wikimedia.org/w/index.php?curid=25088518
37. By Unknown author - Library and Archives Canada does not allow free use of its copyrighted works. See Category:Images from Library and Archives Canada., Public Domain, https://commons.wikimedia.org/w/index.php?curid=26785574
38. By BiblioArchives / LibraryArchives - Library and Archives Canada does not allow free use of its copyrighted works. See Category:Images from Library and Archives Canada., CC BY 2.0, https://commons.wikimedia.org/w/index.php?curid=97701239
39. https://upload.wikimedia.org/wikipedia/commons/f/fe/Operation_Torch_-_map.jpg
40. By Unknown author or not provided - U.S. National Archives and Records Administration, Public Domain, https://commons.wikimedia.org/w/index.php?curid=17335561
41. By USN - Scan from Samuel Eliot Morison: History of United STates Naval Operations in Wolrd War II. Volume II: Operations in North African Waters, October 1942-June 1943. Illustrations between p. 138 and 139. Now in the U.S. Library of Congress, LOC image fsa.8e01526 (see other versions), Public Domain, https://commons.wikimedia.org/w/index.php?curid=6786238
42. https://commons.wikimedia.org/wiki/File:The_Royal_Navy_during_the_Second_World_War-_Operation_Torch,_North_Africa,_November_1942_A12831.jpg#/media/File:The_Royal_Navy_during_the_Second_World_War-_Operation_Torch,_North_Africa,_November_1942_A12831.jpg
43. By fotoreporter sovietico sconosciuto - scan da S.J.Zalova et al, Soviet tanks in combat 1941-1945, Concord publ. 1997, Public Domain, https://commons.wikimedia.org/w/index.php?curid=15947790
44. https://commons.wikimedia.org/wiki/File:Kalac_Novembre_1942.jpg

#/media/File:Kalac_Novembre_1942.jpg
45. https://commons.wikimedia.org/wiki/File:Kusaka_and_Yamamoto_at_Rabaul.jpg#/media/File:Kusaka_and_Yamamoto_at_Rabaul.jpg
46. Public Domain, https://commons.wikimedia.org/w/index.php?curid=1582228
47. By Ewen Montagu Team - Montagu, E.: The Man Who Never Was, London 1953, Public Domain, https://commons.wikimedia.org/w/index.php?curid=15098819
48. By Unknown author - Ben Macintyre: Operation Mincemeat, 2010, Public Domain, https://commons.wikimedia.org/w/index.php?curid=27742985
49. By Unknown author, Public Domain, https://commons.wikimedia.org/w/index.php?curid=2668025
50. https://commons.wikimedia.org/wiki/File:Lockheed_P-38_Lightning_USAF.JPG#/media/File:Lockheed_P-38_Lightning_USAF.JPG
51. By Unknown author, Public Domain, https://commons.wikimedia.org/w/index.php?curid=84628888
52. By Unknown Japanese Press Photographer - The Asahi Shimbun, Public Domain, https://commons.wikimedia.org/w/index.php?curid=120153786
53. By Unknown Japanese Press Photographer - The Asahi Shimbun, Public Domain, https://commons.wikimedia.org/w/index.php?curid=120153785
54. https://commons.wikimedia.org/wiki/File:Operation_Chastise_(the_Dambusters%27_Raid)_16_-_17_May_1943_C3717.jpg#/media/File:Operation_Chastise_(the_Dambusters'_Raid)_16_-_17_May_1943_C3717.jpg
55. By unknown Official RAF photograph - National Archives (AIR 14/840) and IWM HU 69915, Public Domain, https://commons.wikimedia.org/w/index.php?curid=11152059
56. By Flying Officer Jerry Fray RAF - Chris Staerck (editor), Allied Photo Reconnaissance of World War II (1998), PRC Publishing Ltd, ISBN 1571451617, Public Domain, https://commons.wikimedia.org/w/ind

ex.php?curid=2511220
57. By Bundesarchiv, Bild 183-C0212-0043-012 / CC-BY-SA 3.0, CC BY-SA 3.0 de, https://commons.wikimedia.org/w/index.php?curid=5432683
58. By Royal Air Force official photographer - http://media.iwm.org.uk/iwm/mediaLib//8/media-8513/large.jpgThis photograph CH 9720 comes from the collections of the Imperial War Museums., Public Domain, https://commons.wikimedia.org/w/index.php?curid=24469048
59. By Alexpl - Own work, created with en:Inkscape, CC BY-SA 3.0, https://commons.wikimedia.org/w/index.php?curid=9936323
60. By Bundesarchiv, Bild 101III-Merz-023-22 / Merz / CC-BY-SA 3.0, CC BY-SA 3.0 de, https://commons.wikimedia.org/w/index.php?curid=5478220
61. https://upload.wikimedia.org/wikipedia/commons/5/57/Bundesarchiv_Bild_101III-Zschaeckel-207-12%2C_Schlacht_um_Kursk%2C_Panzer_VI_%28Tiger_I%29.jpg
62. https://commons.wikimedia.org/wiki/File:Soviet_M3_Lee_tanks_of_the_6th_Guards_Army_Kursk_July_1943.jpg#/media/File:Soviet_M3_Lee_tanks_of_the_6th_Guards_Army_Kursk_July_1943.jpg
63. By Mil.ru, CC BY 4.0, https://commons.wikimedia.org/w/index.php?curid=58495821
64. By No 2 Army Film & Photographic Unit, Keating G (Major) - http://media.iwm.org.uk/iwm/mediaLib//38/media-38582/large.jpgThis photograph NA 4105 comes from the collections of the Imperial War Museums., Public Domain, https://commons.wikimedia.org/w/index.php?curid=30877673
65. Public Domain, https://commons.wikimedia.org/w/index.php?curid=135394925
66. https://commons.wikimedia.org/wiki/File:The_Invasion_of_Sicily_July_1943_NA4184.jpg#/media/File:The_Invasion_of_Sicily_July_1943_NA4184.jpg
67. By Unknown author or not provided - U.S. National Archives and Records Administration, Public Domain, https://commons.wikimedia.org/w/index.php?curid=17327295

# IMAGES

68. By User:Emanuele Mastrangelo, User:Nederlandse Leeuw - Adapted by Nederlandse Leeuw from Emanuele Mastrangelo&#039;s File:Italian-social-republic-and-civil-war.svg. Note: most texts were written in font Georgia, size 14, not bold. Dates have been corrected to dmy according to military standards., CC BY-SA 4.0, https://commons.wikimedia.org/w/index.php?curid=110835064
69. By Bundesarchiv, Bild 101I-567-1503A-01 / Toni Schneiders / CC-BY-SA 3.0, CC BY-SA 3.0 de, https://commons.wikimedia.org/w/index.php?curid=5412659
70. By Bundesarchiv, Bild 101I-567-1503C-13 / Toni Schneiders / CC-BY-SA 3.0, CC BY-SA 3.0 de, https://commons.wikimedia.org/w/index.php?curid=5412693
71. By ErrantX - Own work using:File:BlankEurope.pngHolt, Thaddeus, The Deceivers: Allied Military Deception in the Second World War (Scribner, New York, 2004) p. 807 - 896, CC BY-SA 3.0, https://commons.wikimedia.org/w/index.php?curid=25249235
72. By War Office official photographer - This photograph H 42527 comes from the collections of the Imperial War Museums., Public Domain, https://commons.wikimedia.org/w/index.php?curid=48098435
73. By United States Army - http://www.psywarrior.com/DeceptionH.html, Public Domain, https://commons.wikimedia.org/w/index.php?curid=4129519
74. Attribution, https://commons.wikimedia.org/w/index.php?curid=228043
75. By Archives New Zealand from New Zealand - Mosquito and crew of the 487 (NZ) Squadron, February 1944, CC BY 2.0, https://commons.wikimedia.org/w/index.php?curid=97703952
76. By RAF - Imperial War Museum - picture scanned by me Ian Dunster 18:58, 18 September 2005 (UTC) from: Mosquito At War by Chaz Bowyer - Ian Allan - 1977 - ISBN 0-7110-0474-9 and credited to: Imperial War Museum.Original uploader was Ian Dunster at en.wikipedia 18 September 2005 (original upload date), Public Domain, https://commons.wikimedia.org/w/index.php?curid=25316276

77. By J.F.M. Trum, Fotopersbureau Gelderland - Dit werk is afkomstig uit de collectie van Regionaal Archief Nijmegen, CC BY-SA 4.0, https://commons.wikimedia.org/w/index.php?curid=65516909
78. By Mike Young at English Wikipedia - Own work, Public Domain, https://commons.wikimedia.org/w/index.php?curid=1646434
79. https://commons.wikimedia.org/wiki/File:IJA_soldiers_during_Operation_U-Go.jpg#/media/File:IJA_soldiers_during_Operation_U-Go.jpg
80. https://commons.wikimedia.org/wiki/File:Evacuaci%C3%B3nDeLiuchowNoviembre1944.jpg#/media/File:Evacuaci%C3%B3nDeLiuchowNoviembre1944.jpg
81. By Imperial Japanese Army - http://www.ww2incolor.com/japan/C___pia+de+7155.html, Public Domain, https://commons.wikimedia.org/w/index.php?curid=52273611
82. By Yomiuri Shimbun - ニュース (9 July 1944), Public Domain, https://commons.wikimedia.org/w/index.php?curid=35032388
83. By Unknown author - Peter Caddick-Adams, Monte Cassino: Ten Armies in Hell, Oxford University Press 2013, ISBN 978-0-19-997464-1., Public Domain, https://commons.wikimedia.org/w/index.php?curid=26493235
84. By Operations Greenwood and Pomegranate Normandy July 1944 EN.svg: Philg88Derivative work: Hogweard - Operations Greenwood and Pomegranate Normandy July 1944 EN.svg, CC BY 4.0, https://commons.wikimedia.org/w/index.php?curid=69750501
85. By US Army - https://laststandonzombieisland.com/2020/06/05/loading-up-76-years-ago-today/, Public Domain, https://commons.wikimedia.org/w/index.php?curid=120119590
86. By Conseil Régional de Basse-Normandie / National Archives USA - http://www.archivesnormandie39-45.org/specificPhoto.php?ref=p011976, Public Domain, https://commons.wikimedia.org/w/index.php?curid=8024584
87. By Chief Photographer&#039;s Mate (CPHOM) Robert F. Sargent, U.S. Coast Guard - Famous Coast Guard Photographs (direct image URL

[1])Also The Coast Guard at Normandy "The Jaws of Death" (direct image URL [2]), Public Domain, https://commons.wikimedia.org/w/index.php?curid=43274

88. https://commons.wikimedia.org/wiki/File:Canadian_landings_at_Juno_Beach.jpg
89. By Evans, J L (Capt), No 5 Army Film & Photographic Unit - http://media.iwm.org.uk/iwm/mediaLib//48/media-48782/large.jpgThis photograph B 5071 comes from the collections of the Imperial War Museums., Public Domain, https://commons.wikimedia.org/w/index.php?curid=24496386
90. By Official U.S. Navy Photograph, now in the collections of the National Archives. - Normandy Invasion D-Day Landings at the Pointe du Hoc, 6 June 1944, Public Domain, https://commons.wikimedia.org/w/index.php?curid=160727
91. By Unknown author - http://www.rsva.ru/rus_guard/2004-06/front-ill.shtml, Public Domain, https://commons.wikimedia.org/w/index.php?curid=2874304
92. By Unknown author - http://www.victory.mil.ru/lib/reel/01/339.jpg, Public Domain, https://commons.wikimedia.org/w/index.php?curid=3247277
93. By Bundesarchiv_Bild_101I-694-0308A-28A,_Russland,_Panzer_IV_und_Transport-Kolonne.jpg: Leherderivative work: Luigi Chiesa (talk) - Bundesarchiv_Bild_101I-694-0308A-28A,_Russland,_Panzer_IV_und_Transport-Kolonne.jpg, CC BY-SA 3.0 de, https://commons.wikimedia.org/w/index.php?curid=11759674
94. By Unknown author - Roman Korab-Żebryk: Operacja Wileńska AK, PWN, Warszawa 1988, ISBN 83-01-08401-4, Public Domain, https://commons.wikimedia.org/w/index.php?curid=10379352
95. By August Ahrens - http://media.iwm.org.uk/iwm/mediaLib//14/media-14956/large.jpgThis photograph HU 86081 comes from the collections of the Imperial War Museums., Public Domain, https://commons.wikimedia.org/w/index.php?curid=36475498
96. By RIA Novosti archive, image #129359 / Michael Trahman / CC-BY-SA

3.0, https://commons.wikimedia.org/w/index.php?curid=15579718
97. By No 5 Army Film & Photographic Unit, Smith D M (Sgt) - http://media.iwm.org.uk/iwm/mediaLib//168/media-168851/large.jpg. This photograph BU 1091 comes from the collections of the Imperial War Museums., Public Domain, https://commons.wikimedia.org/w/index.php?curid=24502300
98. By Malindine E G (Capt), No 5 Army Film & Photographic Unit - http://media.iwm.org.uk/iwm/mediaLib//49/media-49827/large.jpgThis photograph BU 939 comes from the collections of the Imperial War Museums., Public Domain, https://commons.wikimedia.org/w/index.php?curid=24494802
99. By Unknown author - http://www.spaarnestadphoto.nl (Fotonummer SFA003012896), CC BY-SA 2.0, https://commons.wikimedia.org/w/index.php?curid=11871233
100. By Smith (Sgt), No 5 Army Film & Photographic Unit. - Imperial War Museum, Image number BU1109, Public Domain, https://commons.wikimedia.org/w/index.php?curid=16476471
101. By United States Army Air Force - http://www.afhra.af.mil/photos/media_search.asp?q=Airfield&btnG.x=0&btnG.y=0, Public Domain, https://commons.wikimedia.org/w/index.php?curid=12052344
102. By Royal Air Force official photographer - http://media.iwm.org.uk/iwm/mediaLib//54/media-54690/large.jpgThis photograph CL 1811 comes from the collections of the Imperial War Museums., Public Domain, https://commons.wikimedia.org/w/index.php?curid=24455913
103. By Royal Air Force official photographer - http://media.iwm.org.uk/iwm/mediaLib//54/media-54688/large.jpgThis photograph CL 1806 comes from the collections of the Imperial War Museums., Public Domain, https://commons.wikimedia.org/w/index.php?curid=24456093
104. https://commons.wikimedia.org/wiki/File:Royal_Air_Force_Transport_Command,_1943-1945._CL2242.jpg#/media/File:Royal_Air_Forc

e_Transport_Command,_1943-1945._CL2242.jpg

105. By Christie (Sgt), No 5 Army Film & Photographic Unit - http://media.iwm.org.uk/iwm/mediaLib//46/media-46206/large.jpgThis photograph BU 2304 comes from the collections of the Imperial War Museums., Public Domain, https://commons.wikimedia.org/w/index.php?curid=25347717

106. https://commons.wikimedia.org/wiki/File:British_airborne_troops_study_a_sign_outside_Hamminkeln_during_operations_east_of_the_Rhine,_25_March_1945._BU2292.jpg#/media/File:British_airborne_troops_study_a_sign_outside_Hamminkeln_during_operations_east_of_the_Rhine,_25_March_1945._BU2292.jpg

107. By British Government service personnel - Sourced from Norman Franks&#039; Forever Strong 1991 Random Century ISBN 1 36941 102 1 Invalid ISBN.Originally uploaded to EN Wikipedia as en:Image:75 Squadron RMZAF Short Stirling AA-C en route for 26th mission.JPG by Winstonwolfe 3 June 2007., Public Domain, https://commons.wikimedia.org/w/index.php?curid=3127497

108. Public Domain, https://commons.wikimedia.org/w/index.php?curid=3714200

109. By U.S. Navy photo L42-09.06.05, Public Domain, https://commons.wikimedia.org/w/index.php?curid=44651

110. https://commons.wikimedia.org/wiki/File:Explosion_of_the_Japanese_battleship_Yamato,_7_April_1945_(NH_62584).jpg#/media/File:Explosion_of_the_Japanese_battleship_Yamato,_7_April_1945_(NH_62584).jpg

111. By May 3, 2016nik2016 - https://www.alternatehistory.com/forum/threads/operation-unthinkable-what-if.387773/, CC BY-SA 4.0, https://commons.wikimedia.org/w/index.php?curid=94255259

112. https://commons.wikimedia.org/wiki/File:OperationSealion.svg#/media/File:OperationSealion.svg

113. Public Domain, https://commons.wikimedia.org/w/index.php?curid=191289

# Also by Alexander William Emerson

Alexander William Emerson is an author of books on military history and strategy.

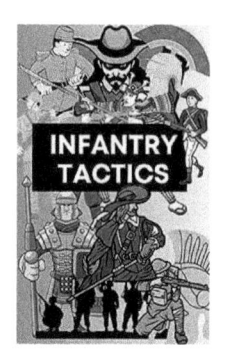

**Infantry Tactics: From Antiquity to the Modern Era**

Are you fascinated by the strategies and tactics that have shaped the course of military history? "Infantry Tactics from Antiquity and Beyond" is your guide to the evolution of infantry tactics from ancient times to modern warfare. With detailed analysis and insights into the tactics of legendary generals such as Napoleon Bonaparte, Frederick the Great, and Oda Nobunaga, this book is a must-read for anyone interested in military history and strategy.

Through compelling narrative, "Infantry Tactics from Antiquity and Beyond" explores how the art of warfare has evolved over the centuries, from the phalanx formations of ancient Greece to the modern fire and maneuver tactics of today's armies. Whether you're a military enthusiast, a history buff, or just looking to gain a deeper understanding of the world around you, this book is an essential addition to your library.

Get your copy of "Infantry Tactics from Antiquity and Beyond" today and discover the fascinating world of military strategy and tactics that have shaped the course of history!

**The World War 2 Book of Trivia**

World War 2 was one of the most catastrophic events in human history, and its impact can still be felt today. If you're a history buff or just curious about this pivotal time in world history, "World War 2 Book of Trivia" is the perfect book for you.

This fascinating and informative book is packed with interesting and little-known facts about the war, from the major events and battles to the behind-the-scenes stories and lesser-known details. You'll discover the incredible feats of bravery and heroism displayed by soldiers on both sides of the conflict, as well as the political and social factors that led to the outbreak of war.

With separate sections for Europe, The Pacific, and each of the major countries in the conflict, "World War 2 Book of Trivia" is a great choice for readers of all ages and backgrounds. Whether you're a history buff looking to expand your knowledge, or simply curious about this important period in human history, this book is sure to captivate and enlighten you. So why wait? Pick up a copy today and start exploring the fascinating world of World War 2 trivia!